A NEW REFORMATION

FROM LUTHER'S WORLD TO OURS

ROB FUQUAY

Abingdon Press / Nashville

A NEW REFORMATION
FROM LUTHER'S WORLD TO OURS

Library of Congress Cataloging-in-Publication data has been requested.
978-1-5018-6401-8

Photos courtesy of Cameron Hershberger

18 19 20 21 22 23 24 25 26 27 — 10 9 8 7 6 5 4 3 2 1
MANUFACTURED IN THE UNITED STATES OF AMERICA

To my father-in-law,
Bishop Richard Wilke,
a relentless reformer

A New Reformation
From Luther's World to Ours

A New Reformation
978-1-5018-6401-8
978-1-5018-6402-5 *eBook*

A New Reformation DVD
978-1-5018-6403-2

A New Reformation Leader Guide
978-1-5018-6410-0
978-1-5018-6411-7 *eBook*

CONTENTS

INTRODUCTION

What do you picture when you hear the word *reform*? I see a rebuilt barn—a barn in southeastern Kansas to be exact.

My wife and I have friends who own the most amazing bed and breakfast called The Barns at Timber Creek located in Winfield, Kansas. Martin and Cheryl Rude's place sits on several acres of beautiful, wooded land. The Barns features two buildings, the main one being Martin and Cheryl's home along with the guest rooms (a guest treehouse also!), and the other, a historic rock barn, which is an event venue.

Along with the peaceful setting, what makes The Barns such a popular retreat is the character of the place. Nearly every piece of the buildings is reclaimed material. One of the barns was about to be demolished (the other practically was, but we'll get to that later). Flooring came from the bleachers in the old fieldhouse at the local college. Each room has a unique barn theme with materials that came from torn-down icehouses, renovated churches, and garbage bins! No wonder people who stay there talk about feeling restored when they leave. The place itself is a picture of restoration!

The Rudes say they have watched many times as families have gathered there for weddings and holidays and relationships have been renewed. One time a pastor came for a personal retreat and stayed in the treehouse room for eight straight days, only appearing for breakfast in the morning. He left refreshed and ready to return to ministry.

For Martin and Cheryl, it's all about story. We are surrounded by stories, stories in the land, the buildings, and each other. Knowing our stories and the stories of the people and things around us reveals how we got where we are. But that's not enough. Our stories are still being told. We are on a journey, which means we are evolving and becoming more than we currently are.

From a faith perspective, we believe that our stories are not our own. The One who gave us a story to tell is telling *his-story* through us. The aim of life is to let our story serve God's bigger story. For this to happen, there must always be reform.

Reform is both challenging and hopeful. It is challenging because change is required. Reform casts a judgment. Something has ceased to serve a purpose, at least as fully as intended. Maybe the times changed. Maybe the people changed. Yet change is necessary for reform to take place. This means more than tweaks. Reform is closer to a total makeover.

Yet reform is hopeful because it means something (or someone!) still has a purpose. As Greg Anderson says, "Having a life mission implies that the world has need of you."[1] Reform keeps the need of a person or thing alive. Without reform, there is simply destruction, whether that destruction comes from a swift decision to do away with something, or the gradual determination to keep things the way they are until fading into obsolescence. With reform, there is hope for continued purpose.

More than five hundred years ago, Martin Luther nailed 95 Theses to the doors of the Castle Church in Wittenberg,

Germany, stating his protest against practices in the Roman Church. There is great reason to believe Luther had no clue about the magnitude of his action. He was not out to take anyone down. He wasn't seeking publicity. He simply felt the time had come for reform in the church he had devoted his life to serving. You must care about something in order to want to reform it. Without care, you just have criticism, like the relative who is glad to point out all the repairs you should make to your house and then leave. Criticism is not reform. Reform means you are ready to roll up your sleeves because you are invested in seeing improvements made.

This is a roll-up-your-sleeves kind of book.

Sure, there will be plenty of history. This book will delve into the major themes of the Protestant Reformation in order to help us understand what shaped the beliefs of the Protestant movement and how we come by many of the doctrines and practices Protestants keep today. Even if you know little of Reformation history, you will learn insights that will enrich and deepen your experience in the church.

This book is hardly an exhaustive coverage of Protestant history. We will not, for instance, study major reformers like Huldrych Zwingli, Martin Bucer, John Calvin, or John Knox. This book exclusively focuses on Martin Luther and the people who shaped his life. Though Luther is popularly identified as the leader of the Reformation movement, you will see how reformation had been brewing for more than a century before him. Luther was more like the person who put the match to a tinder pile that others had been building.

Still, he was a monumental leader. This book will help us relate to Luther and see how his life was a picture of paradox. He was plagued by feelings of inadequacy, yet he was defiant and determined. He struggled with a sense of unworthiness, yet he was confident to the point of being pompous. He experienced bouts of depression that took such a physical and mental toll that he would be incapacitated for weeks, yet he was bold enough to stand before the Holy Roman Emperor and declare, "I cannot recant. God help me. Here I stand!" He rebuked the peasants for their improper behavior, yet Luther was known to curse rapaciously and spoke often in public about the activity of his bowels. Early in his career, he called for an end to violence against the Jews, but late in life he wrote a scathing piece entitled, *On the Jews and Their Lies*. Historians say this publication sowed seeds that bore fruit in Nazi Germany.

What are we to do with such a picture of contrasts? Without embellishing the positives or ignoring the negatives, we let Luther be Luther and recognize that such complexities were simply part of what went into the amazing advancements he made. Luther's fight for equality in the church had huge political implications in Europe and beyond. The Reformation signaled the end of feudalism and was a shot in the arm for democracy. Luther's insistence on the supremacy of Scripture and continuing the work of predecessors to translate the Bible into languages for common people rapidly sped the rate of literacy. Luther did much to advance the role and rights of women when he opened schools to girls. As well, his emphasis on the priesthood of all believers spawned mission and relief efforts for the poor. No doubt you will see how Martin Luther was a complicated individual, but perhaps you will find encouragement for your own inconsistencies and ability to still be used mightily by God.

But this book is not just about history; it is about God's story being told today. Throughout these chapters you will be invited to consider ways the church now is being called to reform. I am United Methodist, and many of the present-day applications are to the church I have devoted my life to serving and which I care about deeply. Like most Protestant churches, The United Methodist Church is facing a multitude of challenges: decline, divisions over sexuality, changes in structure. Some seek to weather the storm by battening down the hatches, riding out the storm, and keeping things the way they are. Others are ready to throw out the baby with the bathwater. My aim is to reform, and that involves both challenge and hope.

Recently our staff had a one-day supervision training with a leader in our church. He spent a little time talking about the word *change*. He said most people are immediately defensive when you talk about the changes they need to make. He recommended using the word *improvement*. Few people resent the idea of getting better, and most welcome the help of those who genuinely care about them. My desire is not to criticize from a distance, but to roll up my sleeves and see what can be done to improve the church. What can we learn from the Reformation five hundred years ago about the New Reformation God is stirring today?

One final aspect of this book will be the personal realm. Reform isn't limited to organizations. In fact, institutional reform is only as effective as the individuals within who are willing to reform. You could say that churches can't reform anything, only the Christians who are a part of them can. Each of us is a work in progress. We always have room to grow. At any given period in our lives, some kind of reform is crying out to be made. What kind of reform might God want to help you make in your life right now? What improvements would you like to see? This book will help you reflect in deeply personal ways about the person you are, the person you are becoming, and where God fits in your story.

If you are reading this book as part of a group study, you will have the opportunity to watch the DVD for each session. This will allow you to visit and experience the places significant in Martin Luther's life. This video was filmed across Europe near the time of the 500th anniversary of the Reformation, and it is a wonderful way to broaden the experience of this study.

As we get ready to begin, let me take us back to Winfield, Kansas. As I was walking around The Barns at Timber Creek, my friend pointed out one of his "fun finds." It was a large, old metal Dr Pepper sign. He said, "I know this may surprise you, but this sign is an antique worth quite a bit of money." I asked how he got it, and he said he found it in a trash dumpster. Then he looked around at his establishment with a longing stare. After a few moments, he broke the silence and said, "You know, I guess you could say that's true for this whole place. Just about everything here was going to be thrown away at one point. Now it all has a new story."

The Protestant Reformation wrote a new story for Christianity and the church. What new stories will reformation write today?

CHAPTER 1
A PERFECT STORM

CHAPTER 1

A PERFECT STORM

It is through living, indeed through dying and being damned, that one becomes a theologian, not through understanding, reading, or speculation.

—Martin Luther[1]

Forming and re-forming. You could say that is God's basic job description. Look at how the Bible begins in Genesis 1, "The earth was formless and empty" (Genesis 1:2 NIV). Then just a few verses later, "the LORD God formed [humankind]" (Genesis 2:7 NRSV). We don't have any specifics on how God formed humanity, but what we do know is that formation was just a beginning. The human body is constantly undergoing reformation.

Scientists have revealed that the body regenerates itself every few years. The 50–75 trillion cells in the body have regenerative ability, meaning that cells are constantly dying. They reproduce so that each part of the body can continue to function and carry out its purpose. For instance, according to British medical experts, the lungs' set of air sac cells basically regenerate every year. Fingernails do about every six months. Every decade we have, in effect, a whole new skeletal system. The only part of the body that does not re-form is the brain.[2] In order for living organisms to continue serving a purpose, they must be re-formed.

Martin Luther was aiming for this kind of reformation when he nailed his 95 theses to the doors of *Schlosskirche*, or Castle Church, in Wittenberg on All Hallows' Eve (October 31) in 1517. He was calling for reforms that would help the church reclaim its core purpose and mission. Specifically, Luther attacked the practice of indulgences. The very first thesis, based on Matthew 4:17, read: "When our Lord and Master Jesus Christ said, 'Repent'…he willed the entire life of believers to be of one repentance." The word translated as repentance in the New Testament is the Greek word *metanoia*, meaning "to change one's mind or direction." To put in modern parlance, Jesus was saying, "It's time to reform." Luther led off his list with Jesus' words about repentance to say it's time for the people, and the church, to reform.

Doors of Castle Church

Luther didn't intend to set off a firestorm. In fact, he posted his theses in Latin in order to address only the university scholars who would be able to understand his words. Luther was calling for a debate on a current hot topic, not an uncommon thing at a university. But the doors of the Castle Church functioned something like today's Internet. They were a place where people posted their opinions and ideas, much like we do with our "posts" on social media. As it turns out, someone took Luther's post and translated his disputation into German. Then a new invention called the Gutenberg press was used to mass produce his 95 protests, and Luther's words went viral. To appreciate why they caused such a reaction, we need to go back at least a century before Martin Luther and understand the complex mixture of forces and tensions mounting in Europe.

The Perfect Storm

The 2000 movie *The Perfect Storm* featured an all-star cast portraying the crew of the ill-fated fishing boat the *Andrea Gail*. In October 1991, the boat sank off the coast of New England in what was described as a meteorological phenomenon. Three different weather systems collided, causing hurricane force winds and tidal wave conditions, all combining to create "the perfect storm."

That's essentially what was happening in Europe in the fourteenth and fifteenth centuries. Three distinct forces collided, setting the stage for major upheaval. These were religious, political, and personal, and each shared a common lightning rod: indulgences. Indulgences were printed certificates sold by the church that granted the buyer release from purgatory or quicker entry into heaven. Understanding this background is critical to understanding what led to the Protestant Reformation.

The Religious Storm

The Protestant Reformation started long before Martin Luther. For a century and a half prior, there had been reformers in Europe like John Hus speaking out against the same abuses and practices Luther would later decry. Hus was the priest of the Bethlehem Chapel in Prague in the early 1400s. His sharpest criticism focused on indulgences.

To appreciate the significance of indulgences, we have to understand purgatory, a Catholic doctrine foreign to most Protestants today. Purgatory came from the belief that the soul must be *purged* before entering heaven, and therefore it first passes through an intermediate state. Add to this belief the very real experience of death. The average life expectancy was thirty-five to forty years old. Frequent plagues and disease could wipe out entire communities. More than half of all children didn't live past infancy. Death loomed large and therefore the church emphasized the afterlife, and very importantly, the role of the church in gaining admission to heaven.

Indulgences served to calm the fears of people. Given all the struggles of this life, especially for peasants, a written guarantee by the church granting release from further struggle in purgatory made indulgences very popular. In fact, the first big business of the Gutenberg Press was printing indulgences, which, in turn, made them a popular source of revenue for the church. A rising number of church leaders like John Hus saw this as an abuse of the church's power and authority. Instead of fueling people's fear of death, the church, in the opinion of these leaders, should be doing more to help people in *this* life. Hus was a true priest who cared deeply about the needs of his parish and the people in his native Bohemia. He began preaching against indulgences and decisions by the pope that seemed to serve the needs of the institution over the people who were part of it.

As a result of his protests, a Church Council was called in 1415 in Constance, where Hus would be tried for heresy. Officials promised a fair hearing, but once Hus arrived, the proceedings moved quickly from trial to sentencing. The bishop who oversaw the proceedings was Johannes Zacharias. It is reported that Hus, whose name means goose, said to the bishop, "You may cook this goose but there will come a swan who will not be silenced." (This is the origin of our expression, "Your goose is cooked.") Hus was burned at the stake on July 6, 1415.

The executioners collected Hus's ashes and threw them into a lake as a symbol of removing Hus's influence. Some of Hus's followers, however, gathered the dirt where his ashes were taken and returned them to Prague, where today a beautiful monument built on the 500th anniversary of his death stands in the city square.

By Luther's time, the practice of indulgences was given unprecedented attention. The pope desperately needed funds to complete the building of St. Peter's Basilica. Vatican representatives were sent throughout the Holy Roman Empire to preach about the importance of indulgences and collect the purchases. The pope even extended the benefits. Release from purgatory was granted not only for those who bought indulgences, but also for loved ones who were deceased. What better way to still be able give to that special someone who has gone before you in death than to provide a direct pass to heaven. Talk about a gift that keeps on giving!

The representative who went to the region of Saxony in northern Germany was Johann Tetzel. He was known for his passionate pleas and effective results in drawing crowds that purchased indulgences. His popular jingle was, "When a coin in the coffer rings, a soul from purgatory springs." It was said that Tetzel even went so far as to claim that if a man had raped the Mother Mary, an indulgence would send him straight to heaven.

Tetzel's role in the community as a carnival-like figure hawking indulgences incensed Luther.

Like Hus a century before him, Luther vehemently spoke out against this practice, and like Hus, he put his life in danger. But before we get to that, let's consider a fundamental question raised by all this: why did people buy indulgences? Why was the mostly poor general population so willing to support such a system? This is where the religious storm combines with the political.

The Political Storm

It was impossible to separate the religious from the political in sixteenth-century Germany. In the fifteenth century, the Holy Roman Empire encompassed all of the German nation. The church and state ruled as one. Various provinces were governed by "electors," who were wealthy local rulers designated by the empire with power to elect emperors. This often put electors in the unique position of being able to curry favor from the Vatican when the pope had a favorite candidate he wanted elected. This was an important reality that would later save Martin Luther's life. The elector of Saxony, Frederick the Wise, interceded numerous times on Luther's behalf using his political favors with the Vatican to protect Luther. Suffice it to say, the church and government were as rife with politics then as now, if not more so!

Even more important to understand is that Europe was still locked in a feudal system. The majority of the population was peasants, and they had no rights. They were denied adequate health care and education. They worked for landowners, most of whom were church officials. Peasants could be beaten and whipped without recourse for disobeying masters. With no ability to fight their case in court, they began to make their voices heard with clubs and swords. Peasant rebellions were appearing more frequently throughout German lands.

For its part, the church tried to preserve the existing social order by emphasizing heaven and Final Judgment. If a peasant class was encouraged to focus on the next life, they might not be as compelled to change conditions in *this* one. Fear of death dominated the art of the times. Paintings adorned the walls of churches showing Christ as Judge sending some to heaven and others to hell. Notice the ones going to heaven do so through the doors of the church! A sort of religious/social codependence had been created. Peasants needed the very institution that preserved the status quo.

Understanding this religious and political climate is key to understanding why the Reformation ignited in the sixteenth century. The peasant culture had grown tired of a church-state that preserved their powerless condition. While they continued to buy into this system by supporting practices like indulgences, more and more voices were speaking out. The brush pile had been laid; all that was needed was for someone to strike a match. This brings us to the third storm.

The Personal Storm

Martin Luther came from a peasant family, something that would always earn him respect and influence with the majority of the German population. He was born on November 9, 1483, in the small village of Eisleben, Germany. He was presented for baptism the very next day at The Church of St. Peter and St. Paul by his father, Hans. Having given birth just the day before, his mother stayed home, understandably! This fact provides further insight to the beliefs and practices of the time. High infant mortality rates meant you didn't take the chance of waiting until the mother could attend in order to make sure the child went to heaven!

21

Shortly after his birth, Luther's family moved from Eisleben to Mansfeld. Luther's father was a miner, though he eventually ascended from the peasant class and became a part owner of a mine. Even with this changed reality, life did not become easier for Martin. His parents were harsh and demanding. His early educational experiences were not easy. His quick wit and temperament often resulted in frequent canings from his teachers. Luther's father was insistent that his son do well in school, and because he was in a position to afford to send his son to university, Luther's father wanted him to become a lawyer. Hans's success meant that Martin would be a respected member of society, perhaps something his father never fully felt about himself. Whatever the reason, upon completion of his primary education, Martin Luther enrolled as a law student at the University of Erfurt.

One summer day in 1505 while walking back to the university following a visit home, Luther was caught in a horrific thunderstorm. He feared for his life and prayed to the patron saint of miners, "Save me, St. Anne, and I'll become a monk." Upon his arrival in Erfurt, instead of going to the university, Luther went straight to the monastery, where at the age of twenty-one, he was admitted to the cloister.

Some scholars question if the storm actually happened, or if it was just a figurative way for Luther to describe his emotional and spiritual state at the time. Two things can be said for sure. Based on the way Luther later wrote about his relationship with his father, attending law school may have been his attempt to earn his father's approval. If this was the case, then no doubt each return to Erfurt would have felt like walking further down a road he didn't want to travel.

Second, Luther was a religious product of his time. He was raised with a healthy fear of God. If pleasing his father was difficult, how much harder was it to please a perfect and holy God who demanded righteousness? If Luther had indeed experienced a literal thunderstorm that summer afternoon in 1505, it certainly fit his inner condition. Literal or figurative, this was a storm God used, and the converging forces in Luther's life and his native Germany were coming together in a way that would forever change history.

> *Often it takes a storm to change conditions keeping us from being all that God wants.... Storms can be purposeful, and the more powerful a storm, the greater the change it brings.*

Today's Storms

Before we go any further looking at this history, let's pause to consider the role and impact of our own storms. What storms do we face today? What are the storms brewing in our nation, in the church, and in your life? Often it takes a storm to change conditions keeping us from being all that God wants. It took a storm to get Jonah to go to Ninevah. A storm led Peter to step out of a boat and walk on water. A storm brought Paul to Malta. Storms can be purposeful, and the more powerful a storm, the greater the change it brings. Storms can be the catalysts of reform.

If the hypothesis at the beginning of this chapter is true, that God is always forming and re-forming, then in order to understand the reformation God seeks now, it may be helpful to consider the storms we face. Let's start with our country. What storms do we face as a nation? What issues are creating fear and uncertainty? In naming these, where do you see Christian faith having application? What would it look like in your church to bring a faith perspective to these matters? Often the issues are so fraught with division there is a fear of even having dialogue. Yet what happens if we don't talk in church about the most important issues of our day? What happens if national and global challenges are devoid of a faith influence? Either we become out of touch and disconnected from the rest of the world or we become fearful of conflict. If nothing else, perhaps naming the ways we are divided and the dangers that exist give a focus to our prayers. Agreeing on what we need to pray about can be the start of reform.

Let's move on to the present-day church. American society is experiencing a dwindling Christian influence. In 1992, only 6 percent of Americans denied having a church preference. Today, about 22 percent of Americans do not claim any church preference. Thirty-five percent of millennials deny having any involvement in church. On the average Sunday, only 17 percent of our population is in church.

According to research from the Barna Group, some of the reasons for decline are the following:

- Distrust of institutions
- Feeling that churches are judgmental and political
- Family makeup is different and many churches struggle to relate to singles, divorced people, same-sex couples, and just about anyone who does not fit the definition of a traditional family

This reality is causing many financial storms in congregations. No longer able to afford staff and programs, some churches are reducing budgets and numbers of employees. Some are even selling their properties and merging with other churches if not disbanding altogether. According to statistics from the General Council on Finance and Administration, The United Methodist Church lost more than 5 percent of congregations between 2011 and 2015 alone!

Other storms appear in the form of infighting. Congregations feeling the need to reach younger people can disagree over the best methods. New forms of worship bring tension over space and values as well as the fear of becoming different congregations within one church. Concerns about changing stands on certain social issues create fear that some may leave and take their money with them.

Is your church facing a storm? Don't just consider *the* church, but your church. Bring the conversation down to your own local community of faith, if you happen to be a part of one. What are the storms threatening change and disruption and the future well-being of your community?

Once you have named your storm, look at it from God's perspective. How might God want to use that storm? Storms always change things. This is the nature of a storm. But if storms, as unpleasant as they may be, bring with them the opportunity to make needed changes, what new possibilities could emerge that help your church to live out its mission?

Karl Barth, a twentieth-century German theologian, found a helpful parallel between the modern church and the story of Jesus and the disciples in a boat during a storm (Mark 4:35-41). Jesus sleeps while the disciples panic. Barth talks about the boat as a metaphor for the church. The boat is rocked and reeled, but it is not going down because Jesus is with them. He writes, "Their apostolic office, their episcopal habits, their experience, their tradition, even the living but sleeping Jesus among

25

them, all appear to be useless. The storm is too violent....But He is in the ship, and for this reason, if for this reason alone, it cannot go down."[3] In other words, our biggest need is to keep our focus on Jesus. How do we do this while also addressing our most pressing problems?

Finally, take the conversation to a personal level. What storms are *you* facing? A divorce? Grief? A health crisis? Conflict? A financial problem? Be specific. Write out exactly what your storm is and how you feel. Without trying to map out a happy ending to your storm, just start by taking your storm to God.

The Protestant Reformation didn't happen because of convincing arguments or rational appeals. The Reformation occurred because people were no longer willing to live with things the way they were. Martin Luther's life was a microcosm of this. His own journey of personal and spiritual misery led him to a breakthrough. Perhaps the biggest need in a storm is to believe that every storm holds the potential for breakthrough. Let's end this chapter thinking about two important principles of spiritual storms.

Storms Are a Sign of God's Presence, Not Absence

What do you typically associate with God's presence, feelings of anxiety or tranquility? I'm not a mind reader, but I'm guessing you're the tranquility type. When most people speak of wanting to have a closer connection with God, they aren't looking for thunder and lightning! Yet notice the way the Old Testament character Job experienced God's presence when he finally had a spiritual breakthrough. For the majority of the book, Job rails against heaven, questions God's judgment, bemoans the day he was born, and asks for one thing: "let me see God's face." At last, Job's prayer is answered, "Then the LORD spoke to Job out of the storm" (Job 38:1 NIV). Rather than serving as a sign of God's absence, a storm held God's presence.

Despite their destructive power, storms not only get our attention, but they also help us to hear from God. As the popular saying goes, "Sometimes God calms the storm; but sometimes God lets the storm rage and calms the child." What if we looked at storms not as hiding God's presence from us, but revealing God's presence to us? What if we listened for God *in* the storm and asked, "Lord, what do you want to say to me in this experience? How do you want to use this storm? What is it I most need?"

Storms Bring Opportunity to Change Something

In 1992, Hurricane Andrew, a Category 5 storm, slammed into Homestead, Florida, flattening nearly every home in its wake. Nearly every home. As it turns out, the houses that fared best were Habitat for Humanity homes. They were built with hurricane strips and other storm-resistant features. As a result of this storm, building codes in Florida changed. Storms always reveal inner conditions.

Jesus once told a parable about this truth. He said, "If you work these words into your life, you are like a smart carpenter who built his house on solid rock. Rain poured down, the river flooded, a tornado hit—but nothing moved that house. It was fixed to the rock" (Matthew 7:25 MSG). Likewise, he said the person who didn't build on a solid foundation experienced complete loss because of the storm. In other words, storms reveal the foundations of life. They show what matters most to us, and not just what we say matters most. Once we are ready to accept that change is imminent and life as it was is not an option, we are open to reform. Reform invites God into our debris to help us build a new life with possibilities the old one did not have.

In 2007, the people of Greensburg, Kansas, experienced an unimaginable tragedy. An EF-5 tornado destroyed the entire town. It was an equal opportunity storm. Everyone lost everything. In the days and weeks following, the people began cleaning up, grieving losses that could never be recovered. Eventually, though, they started to look ahead at how they would rebuild. At a town council meeting residents and officials discussed not just rebuilding but improving. They looked at their plight as an opportunity to build a modern-day town in the most ideal way.

Today, Greensburg, Kansas, has taken great strides to become "green." Residents sought to be eco-friendly and energy efficient in every home, school, church, and civic building. They wanted to be efficient in ways their old town would have never allowed. The new wind turbines alone keep the entire town lighted at night! The people even laugh now about all the years the winds blew across the plains not realizing they contained the energy to power their community!

The mayor said, "You have to do the best you can with the resources you have. We learned that the only true green and sustainable things in life are how we treat each other." He then made this observation about an unexpected benefit of their rebuilding. He noticed many of the new homes have roomy, front porches. He commented, "We need to get back to being front-porch people."[4]

Every storm holds the possibility of reform. Not rebuilding but improving. When life works well for us, we don't tend to see the reforms that could be made. When life doesn't work well for us, we may get so used to the way things are that we simply get stuck. Maybe some storms are a result of our choices. Maybe storms just happen for no fault of our own. But in every storm that comes, God is able to meet us.

As long as there are storms, God will be forming and re-forming.

CHAPTER 2
SOLA SCRIPTURA

Chapter 2
Sola Scriptura

A simple layman armed with Scripture is to be believed above a pope or council without it.

—Martin Luther

In Hoffman, Minnesota, for a little over $10,000, contractor David Gonzalez bought a home built in 1938. Because it needed significant renovation, Gonzales was tearing out walls that had been stuffed with newspaper to insulate the home. While pulling out the paper, he found a first edition *Superman* comic book from June 1938. He thought it could be a valuable collector's item, but he had no idea what it was worth until a buyer in 2013 purchased it for $175,000![1] The find ended up being worth seventeen times what Gonzalez paid for the house. Now that's what I call a fixer-upper!

Reformation is a lot like renovation. It begins with tearing down what has become useless and unnecessary. In the process, valuable things get revealed.

In a similar way, the most significant renovation project in the Bible uncovered an important treasure. During the days of King Josiah, he called for repairs to be made to the Temple. While tearing out old flooring, workers uncovered ancient scrolls. Realizing that what they found was valuable, the workers took the scrolls to King Josiah. Upon hearing the words read aloud, Josiah tore his robes. What did he hear, and why did it cause such a reaction?

The scrolls were the Torah, the Law of Moses. In particular, the king heard the words of Moses warning the Israelites to be faithful to God when they entered the Promised Land. Josiah tore his robes as a sign of repentance as he realized how far his nation had strayed from God's vision.

Let's think about what this story tells us. The people allowed their sacred writings to get buried. Today, when you walk in any synagogue, you see the Torah scrolls front and center before the congregation. They are always in view when the people gather to worship. Yet over many generations in Old Testament history, the people stopped focusing on God's word. Their worship took on other emphases, and eventually the Torah got buried.

The rediscovery launched what came to be known as Josiah's reform. These changes ended child sacrifice and idol worship, reestablished the Mosaic Covenant, and renewed the Passover observance. Second Kings 23:25 provides this assessment: "Never before had there been a king like Josiah, who turned to the Lord with all his heart and soul and strength, obeying all the laws of Moses" (NLT).

In other words, Scripture launched reformation. It always has, then and now.

How Did *Sola Scriptura* Become a Reformation Theme?

One of the principles of the Protestant Reformation was "sola scriptura," or Scripture alone. This became Luther's defense against accusations of heresy. In protesting practices like indulgences, he ended up questioning the authority of the pope, for the pope decreed that indulgences gained their purchasers access to heaven. Luther claimed that such authority is given only by Christ, who supersedes all, even the pope! However, as Christ's representative, the pope holds all earthly authority over the church, and therefore church officials called Luther a heretic, to which he simply responded, "Prove to me in Scripture that I am wrong and I will recant." In so doing Luther established that all authorities of the church were under the authority of Scripture. Thus, "Scripture alone" became an important Reformation theme.

To appreciate how this happened, let's go back and pick up the events of Martin Luther's life where we left off. Following his life-changing thunderstorm experience, Luther entered the monastery in Erfurt. Instead of trying to please his father by becoming a lawyer, he now set out to please God. But if pleasing his father proved difficult, pleasing God would feel nearly impossible. Luther's days in seminary were fraught with anguish, mainly because of his basic proposition of God: because God is holy and we are sinners, we must become holy to be accepted by God. Suffice it to say that Luther was wracked with guilt and a growing sense of helplessness. He spent hours at a time in confession, only to leave and recall some unconfessed thought or deed that would send him running back to confessional. Priests who heard Luther's confessions used to dread his coming. Luther simply felt he could never do enough to be loved and forgiven by God.

Such feelings produced an anguish that Luther described as *Anfechtungen*, a word that doesn't have an exact English equivalent. It is an emotion of anguish or tribulation produced by two opposing forces trying to conquer each other. These feelings often took the physical manifestation of tremors that would come over Luther. This happened at the first Mass he performed as a priest. Luther's father, whom he had not seen since entering the monastery, attended along with about twenty personal guests, all of whom arrived on horseback, meaning they were most likely men of means and importance. This was probably his father's way of showing off his son. If he couldn't bring them to attend a law school graduation, he could at least show them a respected priest conducting Mass. However, the expectation didn't live up to the experience. As Luther raised the loaf to pronounce the words that change the substance of the bread into the body of Christ, he was overcome with a feeling of his own unworthiness. His *Anfechtungen* caused such tremors that he dropped the bread.[2]

His embarrassed father let his feelings show following the service. In front of guests, he accused his son of denying his biblical obligation to honor his father and mother and care for them in their old age. When Luther countered that he was obeying his divine encounter, his father responded, "God grant it was not an apparition of the Devil."[3]

Luther's spiritual anguish deepened further a few years later when he traveled to Rome to represent his monastery at a conference. This was a holy pilgrimage for Luther. For the first time in his life, he was visiting the center of the Catholic Church. He went there expecting to see the church at its best, services conducted in the most sacred of ways, and priests serving out of deep reverence. But if the memory of his first Mass was like an unsettling dream, then his trip to Rome was a nightmare!

At many of the churches in Rome, Luther found priests mumbling through the liturgy as if doing their laundry. The sanctuaries weren't even kept clean. On one occasion, Luther took time at the altar to pray and was admonished by a priest to move along. He even discovered immorality among some priests, astounded that some priests justified sexual infractions because they confined themselves to women.

The trip culminated in his visit to a holy site called the Scala Sancta—or Holy Stairs—believed to be the staircase Jesus climbed to face trial before Pilate. The stairs were brought to Rome by the mother of Constantine. Pilgrims still climb these twenty-eight marble stairs on their knees, and on each step, they recite the Lord's Prayer. In Luther's time, it was believed that if a pilgrim climbed all twenty-eight steps, then a loved one was released from purgatory. Luther got to the top step and said, "Who knows whether it is so?"

Have you ever had similar experiences? Have you ever been disappointed by the church or faith leaders you looked up to? Have you ever had high expectations about the way things should be in the church, only to find the reality falls short?

Luther returned to Germany in personal and professional anguish. His spiritual advisor and mentor was a man named Johann von Staupitz, who often tried consoling Luther with the assurance that God wasn't angry with him, but such efforts didn't seem to help. Returning from Rome, Luther was more frustrated than ever. Soon after this time, Frederick the Wise, the elector of Saxony, founded a university in Wittenberg and asked Staupitz to become the first dean. Staupitz in turn asked his promising young doctoral student, Martin Luther, to come teach and complete his doctoral work. Thinking it might help Luther with his struggles, Staupitz assigned Luther to teach Bible, something Luther protested. He said he didn't have enough time to take on more responsibilities, but one can't help but wonder if Luther's protests had to do with the subject matter. Teaching Scripture would force Luther to confront the God he was starting to dislike. Later in his life Luther reflected on his spiritual state at this time and wrote, "I was myself more than once driven to the very abyss of despair so that I wished I had never been created. Love God? I hated him!"[4]

But it was just this assignment that changed Luther's life. Luther applied himself to this task just like other assignments with his fullest energy and discipline. Over several years, he taught books like Isaiah, Psalms, Romans, and Galatians. He would eventually write and publish commentaries on each of these. During these years, a transformation happened in Luther's heart. Luther was captivated by the idea that Jesus suffered tremendous anguish on the cross, an anguish that caused him to feel forsaken by God. He realized Jesus suffered *Anfechtungen*! Christ could relate to Luther's experience. Words that had long haunted Luther like, "the righteousness of God," were beginning to have new meaning, particularly Romans 1:17 (NIV), "For in the gospel the righteousness of God is revealed—a righteousness that is by faith from first to last, just as it is written: 'The righteous will live by faith.' " Instead of seeing Christ as fearsome judge ready to condemn us for our unrighteousness, Christ is the one who makes us righteous. Our salvation is a gift of faith, not a reward based on good behavior.

Luther was on his way to becoming a new man, all because he took on an unwanted assignment. Can you relate? Have you ever had a breakthrough in faith that came from doing some unwanted activity? Maybe you made a promise to start attending worship regularly or join a Bible study or small group. Perhaps you agreed to serve by teaching a class at church or volunteering at a soup kitchen. Your heart wasn't in it, but along the way a breakthrough occurred. God doesn't rely on our motives in order to bring us to a new place in faith.

No wonder the words *sola scriptura* became a guiding principle of the Reformation. Scripture alone is the way to salvation, not what the church proclaims. If not, then purchasing an indulgence would have probably been enough to put

Luther's conscience at ease. Scripture alone. After all, Luther was a brilliant, well-read scholar. If intelligence alone could produce a liberated soul, then surely Luther would have found a breakthrough sooner. Scripture alone. If not, then Staupitz's counsel would have been enough for Luther. Instead, it was Luther's study of Scripture and the insight he gained to God's grace that liberated Luther from his false understandings of God and enabled him to experience God's grace.

Let's make an important distinction, though. Scripture *alone* does not mean *only* Scripture. Other resources are significant for faith formation. Spiritual writings, mentors, and the tradition of the church all help us grow in our faith. Scripture alone means there is nothing that replaces the role of the Bible as the primary means for hearing God's voice. Scripture became to Luther like an earpiece for hearing God's voice. In fact, he committed for a period of time to reading through the entire Bible twice a year! He was fond of saying that the Bible is like a forest in which he had shaken every branch. Think of that image for a moment. It reminds me of a time I helped a friend harvest apples from his orchard. Sometimes you had to shake the branches in order for the fruit to fall. Hearing God speak to us through Scripture is a similar experience. Like shaking a branch, we must put forth effort to read, understand, and discern what God is saying to us. Such messages come to us like falling fruit.

What Did Scripture Reform?

So, let's think for just a moment about the impact of emphasizing Scripture and how it reformed the church. First, the emphasis on Scripture reformed architecture. The altars in churches, which were all Catholic at the time, were the central, focal point of worship. The Castle Church in Wittenberg, where Luther had the primary preaching responsibilities, reflects this

Inside Castle Church

design. The altar, where the Eucharist was placed, was located at the front of the sanctuary against the wall. The priest conducted the ritual facing the table with his back to the congregation. The Mass was the central event of worship.

The pulpit is practically in the middle of the room to one side. It was not the focal point, and it was no wonder. Many Sundays you might not even have a sermon. The Catholic Church encouraged a homily, or brief sermon, at least once a quarter. Interestingly, today this frequency is reversed in some Protestant churches today where Communion might not be celebrated more than once a quarter but a sermon delivered every Sunday. As well, many Protestant churches place a Bible on the altar table as the focal point of worship and the pulpit takes a more prominent position.

Secondly, the emphasis on Scripture reformed the people. Reformers were passionate about making the Bible available in the common language because of the transformative power of Scripture. Today we can go online or walk into just about any bookstore and find the Bible not only in our language but dozens of versions at that! There are roughly 900 translations and paraphrases of the Bible in the English language alone. It's hard for us to appreciate the sacrifices made to enjoy this freedom. People like William Tyndale gave their lives in the quest to translate the Bible from Latin into the common language. Why? Because they believed that being able to read Scripture for yourself is life transforming, just like it was for Martin Luther. That is why Luther said, "Whoever wants to hear God speak should read Holy Scripture." Luther was fully capable of reading the text in Latin, as well as in the original Greek and Hebrew. While he did not need to read the Bible in German, he wanted to make the life-changing power of the text more easily accessible to common people. Luther's emphasis on *sola scriptura* reformed society. Translating the Bible motivated the common masses to learn to read. As a result, the literacy rate soared in Europe.

Can you remember a time when the Bible became an important resource in your life? I still have the first Bible I was given. It was a Christmas present from my parents when I was a teenager, a leather-bound Bible with my name inscribed on the cover. Seeing my name on the Bible had a profound effect. I didn't just see it as *my* Bible, but as God's Word to and for me. That started a journey to learn and understand Scripture that I am still traveling on today. As someone once said, Bibles shouldn't have back covers so that we remember that God's story continues in the life of every believer. Studying God's story means we understand our own stories even better and realize God's purpose for our lives.

Scripture's Role Today

Given this history of the Bible's importance in Protestantism, it shouldn't be surprising that the Bible is at the heart of division in the church today. Many denominations are embroiled in differences over the right interpretation of Scripture, especially as it relates to passages dealing with human sexuality. On one side of the argument are those who take an orthodox view of the Bible and see verses regarding homosexuality as being incompatible with Christian teaching, or verses defining marriage as between a man and woman as God's clear design.

On the other side are those who take a progressive understanding of Scripture and recognize that the contexts and linguistic differences in many of these passages are good reasons not to interpret them literally and therefore believe these passages do not reflect God's will for all time. They compare the Bible's treatment of homosexuality to issues like slavery, the rights of women, and divorce as examples of how the church changed its views based on a willingness to reinterpret Scripture.

Both sides are vehement in their opinions and the debate raises important questions about the interpretation of Scripture.

What Does the Bible Say About Interpretation?

Second Timothy 3:16-17 says, "All Scripture is God-breathed and is useful for teaching, rebuking, correcting and training in righteousness, so that the servant of God may be thoroughly equipped for every good work" (NIV). What does it mean to say "God-breathed," or as some translations give, "God-inspired"? The process of putting together the books of the Bible in the form we have them today was a very human one. First, before Scripture was ever written, there was the oral tradition, the process of passing along the stories of Scripture verbally. Eventually people began writing the stories as a way to preserve their consistency and accuracy. Then, the process of copying scrolls became very important, and that process was not without controversy. For instance, not all scrolls were copies of original manuscripts, meaning if there were errors in the copies, then such errors were handed down. It's like the old joke about a monk who realized he was copying copies of ancient texts rather than original scrolls. He went to the abbot to point out that if errors got made in the copies, they would be repeated. The abbot agreed that the monk made a good point so he went to the vault to compare current copies with originals. Hours later, the monk heard the abbot wailing from deep inside the vault. When he ran to find out what had happened he heard the abbot lamenting, "It was just one R, that's all, one R. The word was supposed to be CELEBRATE!"

There is no removing human influence in biblical interpretation!

In the early history of the church, councils spent several centuries determining which books should be included in the Bible. Some books were excluded by narrow votes. At the same time, scholars agree that the books we have today are not the only sacred writings. As well, Pauline scholars believe Paul wrote more letters than we have preserved, such as three or possibly four additional letters to the Corinthian Church. What if these lost documents contain statements that dispute those we have in the Bible?

Such questions are really senseless. It's like trying to admit evidence in court that doesn't exist. You just can't do it. What we get is the recognition that the words "God-breathed" mean more than God dropping the Bible out of heaven into our laps. There are just too many complexities and variances in Scripture to fairly interpret the Bible in a literal way. For instance, there are contradictions within Scripture itself. In one place, the Bible says God punishes children for the sins of their parents (Exodus 34:7); yet in another it clearly says this is not the case (Ezekiel 18). Jesus says two very different things about people who are indifferent toward him. In one place he says, "Whoever is not with me is against me" (Matthew 12:30 NIV).

41

Yet in another, he says, "Whoever is not against us is for us" (Mark 9:40 NIV).

The Bible is hard to interpret literally, but when we understand the different contexts and authors and reasons for writing, we discover meaning in spite of the differences. In other words, the Bible demands that we exercise interpretive discernment in which we look at individual verses against the wider view of God's will revealed in all of Scripture and particularly the Spirit of Jesus. This is why we don't execute rebellious children today like the Law of Moses required, and why the father of the prodigal son would have been scandalous in his mercy. The example of Jesus compels us to interpret Scripture based on what it means to practice God's love and live true to God's will given what we know in our situation.

Still, some fear that if we change our interpretation of what seem to be clear biblical mandates, we are throwing out the baby with the bathwater. They claim this weakens all of biblical authority. Let's be even more specific. What do we do with this pesky issue of sin? Either sex outside of a heterosexual relationship is a sin or it isn't, right? The answer is simple if you interpret the Bible literally. It is not so simple if you practice interpretive discernment. For instance, look at the two references to homosexuality in Leviticus. Chapter 18 places it (verse 22) among a long list of sexual perversions that are abolished. Yet by chapter's end the real issue seems to be about separating the Israelites from other cultures that worshiped false gods (verse 24). That is, condemnations against homosexuality were about distinguishing the Israelites as followers of Yahweh. In Leviticus 20, homosexuality is clearly forbidden in verse 13, punishable by death! But the same warning and punishment is also given for children who curse their parents (verse 9). Clearly, we don't look at these two the same today, yet they are treated identically in the Bible.

Therefore, if using such examples of interpretative discernment might mean that homosexuality is not a sin, does that mean we should disregard all examples of sexual standards mentioned in Leviticus 18 and the rest of Scripture? Of course not! It means we practice discernment like the apostles did in Acts 15, seeking to understand what is God's will regarding a particular issue without throwing out all standards completely.

Coming to a new and different insight of God's will by reinterpreting Scripture is part of our religious tradition. Even Jesus did this in the Sermon on the Mount when he said he did not come to abolish the Law but fulfill it (Matthew 5:17), and then began listing numerous reinterpretations of Mosaic Law saying, "You have heard that it was said... but I say to you" (Matthew 5:21-48 NRSV). Openness to a new interpretation of the Bible is being faithful to the authority of Scripture, not unfaithful.

If the church had locked in its interpretation of Scripture and excluded Gentiles in Acts 15, we probably wouldn't have a church today. If the church had locked in its understanding of the role of women and continued to refuse positions of leadership based on gender, we would not have a church as healthy as we do now. If the church had locked in an opinion that slavery should be legal because the Bible doesn't prohibit it, then our entire society would be corrupt. Reinterpreting Scripture is not just acceptable, it is a moral responsibility.

God uses Scripture to right injustices,
advance equality, and breathe
hope into weary souls.

Scripture launches reform, and God is always reforming nations, churches, and individuals that reflect the values we see in the life of Jesus. Instead of removing people from that grace and hope, God uses Scripture to right injustices, advance equality, and breathe hope into weary souls.

I never cease to be amazed at how God uses Scripture to change lives. I have preached passages of the Bible that talk about forgiveness and later hear from someone who was inspired to forgive another. I've heard people talk about reading passages of Scripture that convicted them about changes they needed to make or commitments to serve or give as a response of obedience. God still breathes through Scripture. Our role is to help greater numbers of people experience God's breath of hope. Just ask Andrew Dollard.

Andrew is a member of my church. Several years ago, he was wrongly accused of something that cost him his job, his marriage, his home, and most of his possessions. Though he was eventually acquitted of any wrongdoing, the damage was done. Sitting on his bed one day, he contemplated taking his life. He looked over at the night table and saw his Bible collecting dust. He opened it to Philippians and read Paul's words, "I have learned to be content whatever the circumstances." He learned how Paul most likely wrote those words in jail. Andrew felt that Paul understood his experience. This led Andrew to seek the source of Paul's contentment and give his life to Christ in order to renew his faith.

Sola scriptura. There is nothing that replaces the power of God's living and active Word. Why did Reformers risk and even give their lives so that a simple book could be translated? So that a guy like Andrew Dollard could one day get his life back! So that all people can know they have a place in the family of God and can have the peace of God through Jesus Christ.

CHAPTER 3
SOLA FIDE

CHAPTER 3
SOLA FIDE

Most of us were taught that God would love us if and when we change. In fact, God loves you so that you can change.
—Richard Rohr

Then I grasped that the justice of God is that righteousness by which though grace and sheer mercy God justifies us through faith. Thereupon I felt myself to be reborn and to have gone through open doors into paradise.
—Martin Luther

I'll never forget the experience of grace at a football game. I was in college and had gone one weekend to visit a friend who attended a large university. That Saturday, we went to a football game, something that was exciting to me because my college didn't even have a football team! My friend explained that students at the university got in free with their student IDs. He said, "I got you covered." His out-of-town roommate had left his ID for me. I started to ask if this was legal, but fearing the answer, I kept quiet. I assumed I could always plead the fifth—that is, to answer like a five-year-old, "I didn't know!"

He coached me to put my thumb over the picture, stay close to the group, and flash the ID fast. Sure enough, it worked. We got seated well before the game started. Being colder than I thought, I told my friend I was going back to the dorm to get a jacket. He said, "You don't want to push your luck. You better stay here."

I said, "You kidding? That was a snap. I'll be back in 20."

On my return entry, there was a different gatekeeper, someone who took his job much more seriously. I did the ol' thumb-over-the-picture routine, flashed the ID, and the guard said, "Wait a minute, let me see that card." With careful inspection he said, "This doesn't look like you." I explained that I had a haircut since that picture. It would have helped had I taken time to notice the guy in the picture had a crew cut! "Really?" the guard replied, "Then tell me your home address." After I stuttered a couple of times, he handed me back the ID (thankfully he didn't keep it) and told me, "You'll have to buy a ticket."

Now I had a problem. I had just enough cash to buy gasoline to get home. I got in line to make my purchase wondering how I was going to afford a ticket and gas money. I was the next person in line to the counter when a man walked up to me and asked, "Want a ticket for the game?"

I responded disbelievingly, "Sure."

He said, "I have an extra. Enjoy." And he walked off.

I rejoined my friends, enjoyed the game, was able to drive home that night, and realized what it is like to experience grace. Could that be a fair description of our spiritual condition? We stand on the outside of the metaphorical gates of heaven because of our own foolish mistakes and wrongdoing. We have no idea how we can ever afford admission. And along comes a man, who for no good reason other than his good nature, grants us entrance. Martin Luther never watched a football game, but he did hold that same ticket.

Salvation by faith through grace was another key theme of the Reformation. If nailing the 95 Theses to the doors of the Castle Church in Wittenberg was the political cannon shot that launched the Reformation, then the theological banner of the movement was justification by faith. This became known as *sola fide*, faith alone, because what saves us is not our works but God's grace, which we receive by faith. This is how we are made right with God. But why was grace such a radical concept?

What Made Grace So Radical?

As mentioned in the last chapter, Martin Luther had a propositional faith such that he believed he must be deserving of God's grace. Luther was a mere product of his environment, one that had been shaped for thousands of years by the philosophy of Aristotle, particularly two key ideas.

The first is Aristotle's famous phrase, "Like is known by like." Through the ages this statement influenced theological thinking in the following way: we are spiritual beings and therefore made for fellowship with God. However, fellowship with God can take place only when the sinner is raised to likeness with God. God is holy so the sinner must become holy in order to be saved. Becoming holy is the job of the sinner, which leads to a second influential idea of Aristotle's.

"Practice makes perfect." Believe it or not, that sentence didn't originate with a piano teacher. And, while Aristotle also cannot take credit for it, the phrase did factor significantly into his understanding of habits. The more you work at developing a skill or practice, the better you will be. Hence, the more we work at holiness, the holier we will become.

49

By Luther's day, these two ideas came together in the form of a very popular saying, "Do what lies within you." On the surface, this sounds encouraging. Do the best you can and you will be accepted. But in theological use, the idea can have a troubling consequence, especially for a spiritually sensitive young man like Martin Luther. How can you know if you have done your best? How can you know that you really did everything possible in order for God to associate with you? If doing what lies within you means that salvation includes some element of human performance, what if you could have or should have done more?

This is why Luther used to spend long hours in confessional. He was so conscious of the need to do his best that he couldn't afford to leave anything unconfessed. Not everyone would have been as troubled as Luther. In fact, most people probably didn't ponder these ideas too deeply. But for someone who did, like Luther, and anyone who was deeply devoted in faith and most concerned about living the right way, this cultural theology produced deep anguish. It makes me think of Paul's words in Philippians where he reflects on his life as a Pharisee. He was raised in a similar religious world with a similar commitment to doing things right. He wrote,

> *If anyone else has reason to be confident in the flesh, I have more: circumcised on the eighth day, a member of the people of Israel, of the tribe of Benjamin, a Hebrew born of Hebrews; as to the law, a Pharisee; as to zeal, a persecutor of the church; as to righteousness under the law, blameless.*
>
> *Yet whatever gains I had, these I have come to regard as loss because of Christ.*
>
> (Philippians 3:4-7 NRSV)

Luther made a similar observation of his life as a young man saying, "If ever a monk could have reached heaven by his monkery, it is I."

What about you? Ever tried to reach heaven by your own *monkery*—things you were taught you had to do to be accepted by God? Can you look back and see any grace snags from the religious environment in which you were raised? Maybe a religion with a lot of rules, or a belief that God was angry with you and you could never measure up? What obstacles to grace do you find yourself still trying to overcome?

For Martin Luther, the politics of his day did not help the situation. In a still dominant feudal system of haves and have-nots, typically the church officials represented the haves. The church's theological emphasis became a useful way of preserving the status quo. At a time when life expectancy was thirty-five to forty years old, the church emphasized preparing for the next life. Since the path to heaven led through the doors of the church, so the thinking went, then the key was living in such a way that God would accept us. No wonder indulgences played well. They provided a clear strategy for earning salvation and kept the economy of the Holy Roman Empire strong at the same time.

However, for one young monk in a tiny village in Germany, this whole system brought him to a breaking point while sitting in his study tower one day. So let's pick up the events of Martin Luther's life from where we left off in the last chapter.

Luther's Protest

After he became dean of the new University of Wittenberg, Johann von Staupitz, Luther's mentor and superior, assigned Luther to teach Bible. During this time, the pope called for a new emphasis on selling indulgences, and as we learned in chapter 1, Johann Tetzel was the Vatican emissary who preached in villages near Wittenberg. When Luther started seeing many of the Wittenberg citizens showing off their certificates of indulgence, a dam broke inside him. Having given his best to a system of works righteousness that failed to bring him closer to Christ and now seeing people prop up a religion that didn't really care for their well-being, Luther felt the time to act had come.

He wrote a list of protests calling into question the practice of indulgences. He waited to post them until All Hallows' Eve, October 31, because this was an annual day to promote superstitious rituals such as the viewing of relics. Wealthy owners of such items, like the elector of Saxony, Frederick the Wise, would present the items he possessed to people in Wittenberg, who could pay money to see them, providing further revenue for him and the church. Some of these relics supposedly included a twig from the burning bush Moses saw, thorns from Jesus' crown, hay from the manger,[1] bone fragments of saints, and more.[2]

Luther's timing risked offending Frederick, and this could be a dangerous move since Frederick built the University of Wittenberg and paid Luther's salary! Luther was discreet. He posted his list in Latin, seeking merely to call for a debate among scholars. Obviously, Luther's words were scandalous. His action was bold. The reaction would no doubt be explosive. Luther nailed his list to the doors of the Castle Church, and... *crickets*! No response. Perhaps a yawn or two at best from passersby who took time to read the first three or four items and moved on.

The truth is, what Luther said wasn't all that novel. There were others questioning practices like indulgences and the decisions of the pope, but what made Luther's words unique was the way he expressed his ideas with passion. In fact, the only reason we know about Luther's 95 Theses, and perhaps the reason we even have a Protestant Church today, is because of someone we don't even know who took Luther's post, translated it, published copies, and distributed them around northern Germany. That's when Luther's words went viral.

In the next chapter, we will pick up the story from there. For now, our attention is on the other activity happening behind the scenes in Luther's life. In fact, this other activity was even more important because it led to the spiritual breakthrough we discussed in chapter 2. There's no way to fully separate the themes of *sola scriptura* and *sola fide* as they were part of the same experience. The study of Scripture is what led to Luther's experience of grace, but the significance of both and the impact on the movement of the Reformation demand separate attention.

A Towering Experience

Day after day, Luther studied in a room in the tower at the university preparing for Bible classes. Before he nailed the 95 Theses to the church doors, Luther had his spiritual breakthrough. He referred to it as his "tower experience." Gradually putting together years of insights and learning from Scripture, there came a moment when his heart was changed. God's grace broke through. This was not just an intellectual

Luther's Study Tower

insight. Luther was flooded with the experience that his good works were not the basis for his acceptance by God. He didn't have to earn approval. He finally had peace with God.

Nearly 200 years later, an Anglican priest named John Wesley would suffer the spiritual anguish of trying to merit God's favor. He came under the influence of Moravians, descendants of John Hus, whose life and death influenced Martin Luther. The Moravians spoke with Wesley about the need for personal experience in faith and the assurance of Christ's love and forgiveness. Wesley deeply yearned for this experience, but how could he have it? One night at a Moravian gathering on Aldersgate Street in London, Wesley felt his heart strangely warmed as he listened to a reading of Luther's Preface to Romans. As a United Methodist, I am very familiar with this story, but not until a few years ago did I actually read Luther's Preface that Wesley would have heard. Here is just a small portion of what Luther wrote:

> Faith is not what some people think it is. Their human dream is a delusion. Because they observe that faith is not followed by good works or a better life, they fall into error, even though they speak and hear much about faith. "Faith is not enough," they say, "You must do good works, you must be pious to be saved." They think that, when you hear the gospel, you start working, creating by your own strength a thankful heart which says, "I believe." That is what they think true faith is. But, because this is a human idea, a dream, the heart never learns anything from it, so it does nothing and reform doesn't come from this 'faith,' either....Faith is a living, bold trust in God's grace, so certain of God's favor that it would risk death a thousand times trusting in it. Such confidence and knowledge of God's grace makes you happy, joyful and bold in your relationship to God and all creatures. The Holy Spirit makes this happen through faith.[3]

What parts of those words stand out to you? Frankly, for many Protestants today, especially those who have been in churches all their lives, believing in *sola fide* is typically not a problem. The idea that we depend on grace, not our actions, for salvation is not problematic. What many people may share with Luther and Wesley, however, is the need to experience this truth. Luther and Wesley spent years studying the role of grace through faith. They understood this belief, but it was their experience of God confirming it in their hearts that transformed them. Have you ever had such an experience of faith? As Wesley was asked, "Do you have the assurance that your sins are forgiven?" Do you have a Tower Experience or an Aldersgate Street where the reality of God's love exploded in your heart, something so real that you would say with Luther it's worth risking death a thousand times trusting it?

We'll come back to those questions at the end of the chapter. Right now, let's consider some implications of this central doctrinal principle of the Protestant Reformation.

Justification by Faith

Paul's declaration that we are "justified by faith" in Romans 5 seems so clear and simple it is hard to imagine a time when these words were revolutionary. Yet when the general populace couldn't read Scripture for themselves, and the head of the church declared that we must merit salvation, we might appreciate how Luther's study of this phrase led to something glorious. Getting there, however, was not a fast journey.

Luther had long wrestled with the concept of the justice of God. How can anyone live up to God's justice? It was like a card game with the dealer offering a no-win hand. But Luther's persistent study led to a breakthrough. He realized that *justice* is the root of *justification*. We can be justified before God, not because we meet God's justice, but because Christ offers it. This is what makes Christ a judge; he has the power to declare us just through his work on the cross by which he took away our punishment.

But what happens to sin? If like is known by like, does the acceptance of Christ's sacrifice on the cross mean sin is removed? Then, as now, you need only observe the behavior of Christians to know that sin sticks around!

The Latin phrase Luther used to deal with this paradox was *simul justus et peccator*, "at the same time righteous *and* a sinner." This concept was what made Luther's treatment of justification by faith radical for the time. His knowledge and study of ancient languages helped him arrive at this idea. He started with the Latin word for justification, *justificare*, which comes from *Justus*, meaning—as you might guess!—justice; and *facare*, meaning to make. Next, he took the original Greek that Paul used, *dikaiosis*, which means to regard as just or righteous, or to pronounce acquitted in a legal sense. This was a slight but very important distinction for Luther.

The Latin understanding had created a sense in which justification was something made to happen. Through the Mass, which was literally a sacrifice performed on the altar each week, as well as other works, we are made righteous before God. In the Greek though, Luther realized justification is passive, not active. We are justified by God because of what God has done, based on no merit of our own. Simply by faith alone, which remains a gift of God, we receive this "alien righteousness," as Luther called it. The righteousness of Christ is what saves us, not our own righteousness. Sin is not removed. We are loved and accepted by God in our sin.

A good illustration is found in the latest invention of Luther's time, the Gutenberg Press. For the first time, an automated

56

printing machine justified the margins of a page; that is, it put each line in perfect alignment. We are like the words on a page, unable by our own ability to be justified, but we depend on the power of God, who like a Master Printer, puts us in right alignment. If there is any work on our part, it is to trust and accept this power and gift.

This is what led Luther to offer some pretty audacious advice to a friend suffering from the same struggles Luther did earlier in his life. The friend had a hard time trusting in this grace and resisting his human need to earn his acceptance. Luther told him to sin boldly but trust Christ more boldly still! While such advice could easily be misconstrued, Luther was simply saying, quit trying to resist your humanity and berating yourself for your imperfections. Our sins, instead of driving us to despair, drive us to Christ, who gives us the assurance that we are justified while yet in our sins.

What does this mean for the church today? How well does your congregation do at helping people experience this reality of grace? Is your church a comfortable place for people who already have this assurance, or is it a community that makes it clear people who don't feel worthy of God's love have a place? What does your church do to let people know they are welcomed as they are?

What does your church offer to help people make this discovery? Neither Luther nor Wesley found peace because someone told them God loved them. They both had to work at it. What a paradox! They discovered they didn't have to earn God's love by engaging in the work of study and prayer.

Some discoveries come only through struggle. To eliminate the challenge can eliminate the breakthrough. I think about my adult children. When they hurt, my wife and I hurt. We feel the temptation to step in and run interference for them. But we both know there are discoveries and growth that come as a result of struggle.

As a church, we don't want to cause people to struggle, but what do we do to help them in their struggles beyond kind words and platitudes? Remember, Luther's breakthrough came when Staupitz gave him an assignment to teach Scripture. Does your church offer learning opportunities in an environment that is friendly to people who are learning? Do you offer faith exploration classes? Do you promote retreats that have been faith-renewing to longtime church members? Perhaps the New Reformation in your church will happen when your administrative board or staff leadership gets away for a weekend to answer: How well is our church helping people experience transformation in their faith, and what more can we offer?

> As a church, we don't want
> to cause people to struggle,
> but what do we do to help
> them in their struggles beyond
> kind words and platitudes?

Anguish Is a Plea, Not a Verdict

Remember our word *Anfechtungen*? It doesn't translate well into English, but it's the word Luther used to describe his anguish with God, his feeling that he could never do enough to please God. As he would discover, though, this feeling of anguish wasn't a verdict on his condition. It was more like a plea, motivation to keep seeking the truth about God and himself. As he kept wrestling with God, this anguish was what brought him to the truth, that he is put right with God through faith.

One of Luther's favorite Bible stories was Jacob wrestling with the angel in Genesis 32. Jacob wrestled all night and by morning's light, the story says he prevailed in his struggle with God. For Luther, this story was liberating. Jacob prevailing against God did not mean he somehow defeated God, but rather he had defeated his own false assumptions about himself and his relationship with God. Because he was willing to take his struggle to God and not give up, he emerged a new man.

The word *Anfechtungen* is about the anguish experienced from struggling with another. Luther came to realize his struggle wasn't really with God but with himself and his own false beliefs and ideas about what he had to do to deserve acceptance. This makes a helpful point for us when we are tempted to render a verdict on ourselves because of our feelings of unworthiness. Such feelings are pleas, not verdicts. They are meant to keep us searching and wrestling with God because feelings of unworthiness are not from God.

The Jacob story ends with Jacob receiving a new name, Israel. Likewise, Luther, after his breakthrough of justification, changed his name. His last name was actually Ludher. Now Martin gave a slight variation playing on the name Eleutherius, which means "free one." He became Martin Luther when he was finally free.

Many years later, another young boy would receive a similar name change. An American Baptist pastor, Michael King Sr., took a trip to Europe, where he studied the life of Martin Luther. He became so inspired by Luther's courage he decided to change his name, but what about his five-year-old son who was named after him? Like father, like son, and that is how Martin Luther King Jr. got his name. God uses transformed people to transform people.

Grace Is an Experienced Reality

Grace must always go beyond mental assent to personal experience. In fact, you could say that we come to believe in grace as a result of experiencing it.

Perhaps the greatest reform needed in the church is the easiest to enact, simply showing grace to all people. What would your church look like if members defined what a revolution of grace would mean? Such a revolution would happen by simply answering questions like these:

- What are the experiences you want to make sure people have when they come to your church?
- How do you want people to feel after attending a worship service or event at your church?
- What can you do to show people they matter to you?
- Do people feel loved in your church as they are or as you want them to be?

We come to believe in grace when we have experienced grace.

This past year, one of our members spoke in worship. He just so happened to be a very well-known figure in professional sports. Something funny but sad happened. He sat with his wife a few rows back from the front waiting to be called up at the time of the message. Our members knew he was speaking in worship, so we had a packed house. Just before the service started, a woman came up to him and said, "I'm sorry, can you sit somewhere else. Don't you know who is speaking today? I've saved these seats for my family." He chuckled to himself, said, "No problem," and moved to another spot.

What would it look like to practice a revolution of grace where members act like visitors and treat visitors like VIPs?

Could a simple revolution of grace turn around the decline in churches today? It's worth a try finding out.

Faith alone, grace alone. Together they make a New Reformation for the church.

CHAPTER 4
TAKING A STAND

CHAPTER 4
TAKING A STAND

My conscience is captive to the Word of God. I cannot and will not recant anything, for to go against conscience is neither right nor safe. God help me. Here I stand. Amen.
—Martin Luther

I appeal to Jesus Christ, the only judge who is almighty and completely just. In his hands I plead my cause, not on the basis of false witnesses and erring councils, but on truth and justice.

—John Hus

When my daughters were little girls, I wanted them to be confident and independent so they didn't go along with the crowd...until they actually became confident and independent.

I remember a time when two of them were small and got into an argument. We were in our van. One reacted to something the other did by hitting her. I demanded an apology from the defendant to the plaintiff, reminding her how the law reads: "No matter what, we don't hit each other." There was a long silence. So I did what any determined parent would do. I used blackmail. "If you want a Dilly Bar at Dairy Queen, you will tell your sister you're sorry." Finally, a response, the most sarcastic "I'm sorry" you can imagine. I said, "No good. You have to mean it." Again, a half-hearted reply. "You can do better than that," I demanded. She let out a huff. Then a grunt. And finally, an acceptable, "Sorry."

We drove in silence, and then we pulled up to the Dairy Queen. We got our Dilly bars and headed back to the van. As the accused daughter got into the vehicle, she informed me, "I had my fingers crossed when I apologized!"

The greatest force in the world is the strength of the human will. Authority can use its force to hear the words it wants, but it cannot silence a person's voice. Standing before the rulers who could take his life if he did not say the words they wanted to hear, Martin Luther defiantly stood his ground and said, "I cannot recant." He didn't have to cross fingers.

Big Shoes to Fill

In preparation for the five hundredth anniversary of the Protestant Reformation, the city of Worms in Germany created a remembrance path in the place where Martin Luther made his defiant stand before the powers of the Holy Roman Empire. One station has large metal shoes in the place where Luther stood when asked by the emperor to recant his claims questioning the authority of the pope and the teachings of the church. You can step into the shoes and imagine what it was like for Luther to say, "I will not recant...here I stand!"

Standing in Luther's shoes brought a mixture of intimidation and inspiration for me. I thought about the courage it must have

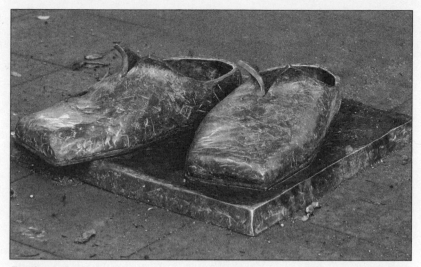

Replica of Luther's shoes

taken to speak words of defiance to the very authorities you once devoted your life to obeying, not to mention the fact that those words would put your entire life in jeopardy. At the same time, I was inspired by a legacy of courage that shaped my life as a Protestant Christian today. This act of defiance changed history. I was reminded that the bigger the change or reform needed, the greater the courage that will be required. Whether we are talking about issues in our nation, our workplace, our church, or our personal lives, reform must be accompanied by an equal measure of courage.

To appreciate the significance of this event and the lessons it holds for us today, we need to understand how Luther got from Wittenberg to Worms.

From Wittenberg to Worms

Luther's first defiant stand was nailing his 95 Theses to the Castle Church doors in Wittenberg. Granted, that wasn't like thumbing your nose at the Holy Roman Emperor, but it was

67

a stand. Big, defiant stands often start with smaller ones. We admire the courage of Polycarp, the second-century bishop who refused to deny Christ and was executed; or John Hus, who refused to recant his critique of church practices and was burned at the stake; or nearer our day, Archbishop Oscar Romero, who defended El Salvador's poor against nefarious powers and was gunned down while saying Mass. We revere such heroism and at the same time tremble at the thought of doing the same. Hopefully we will never have to stand in their shoes. But let's not forget that big courage starts small. Martin Luther was a simple, insecure monk of peasant lineage who was growing in his confidence to speak out. He was most likely propelled not by his self-confidence but by the cause churning inside him. He was incensed by the church's power and abuse.

That's where courage begins, with conditions we know in our soul must be changed. Take a moment right now to think about any issues you feel must be changed. Do you know of anyone being unfairly treated? Do you know of people who don't get the same opportunities as others? Do you know of an injustice going on? What do you believe deep in your soul that God would want different?

It's easy to talk ourselves out of taking any steps because we wonder what difference we can make, but again, think of Luther. All he did was nail a list to a door. Big change starts small.

Of course, Luther would soon find himself taking many more steps. Coming somewhere in the middle of his own spiritual breakthrough, Luther's decision to post his 95 Theses barely drew a yawn from his intended audience—university scholars. However, when his post was translated into German, Luther became an overnight sensation. This led to reactions from Rome. At first Pope Leo X brushed it off, saying, "Luther is a drunken German. He will feel differently when he is sober." This was one of the greatest miscalculations in history. His error in judgment, however, would soon change.

As Luther preached and published his opinions, new stands would be required. The next big one was in the spring of 1518 when he participated in a disputation in Heidelberg. It was here that a Dominican priest from Strasbourg named Martin Bucer first heard Luther and became an avid follower. No doubt Bucer heard views that resonated with his own and sparked a passion within him. Have you ever heard someone who makes you say, "I've had those same ideas and opinions; I've been thinking those exact thoughts!"? Bucer must have felt this way in listening to Luther. In following years, he arranged for his monastic orders to be annulled and was excommunicated from the Catholic Church for advancing heretical beliefs.

This provides another meaningful reflection. Think of the impact of someone taking a stand. Someone's example inspires people. The courage of one fuels the flames in others. What people in your life inspire you by their bold stands? How do you influence others by your willingness to take a stand? How do your children, colleagues, or friends see courage in you?

Luther's conviction continued to help him win new friends like Andreas Karlstadt and Philip Melanchthon, both of whom would be important partners in the Reformation movement. However, new foes emerged as well. The more Luther spoke and published, the more the Vatican was compelled to act. In the summer of 1518, court actions were taken against Luther summoning him to appear in Rome for trial. His friend, the elector of Saxony, Frederick the Wise, interceded on Luther's behalf, prevailing upon the Vatican to allow Luther to be interrogated on German soil. Therefore, in the fall of 1518, Luther appeared before Cardinal Cajetan in Augsburg. The reputation of Luther's rhetorical skill must have spread, because Cajetan was ordered not to debate Luther but to extract a statement recanting his views. If Luther refused, Cajetan was to bring him bound to Rome. Luther lured Cajetan into debate, refused to recant, and managed to escape by night back to Wittenberg.

Obviously, boldness was growing in Luther, but his life was clearly in danger. Fortunately, the threat against Luther found temporary reprieve due to unforeseen circumstances. The Holy Roman Emperor, Maximilian, died in January 1519. The pope needed the support of Frederick the Wise to get his candidate King Charles of Spain elected as the new emperor. In exchange for that support, Frederick was able to negotiate a truce for Luther. The art of politics is knowing the right time to call in favors!

For most people, this would be a good time to stay out of public view, but that's most people. Not Martin Luther! That summer, he participated in a highly anticipated debate in Leipzig against Johann Eck, creating yet more attention. Luther had tremendous respect for the intellect and debating skill of Eck, a fellow German. While the debate was considered a draw, Eck scored points by identifying Luther with John Hus of a century before, even labeling Luther "the Saxon Hus." This image pegged Luther as an opponent to the authority of the pope, a characterization Luther would need no help advancing. Soon enough, Luther was publicly calling the pope the Antichrist!

During this time, Luther published what would prove to be the fatal blow in his growing war with Rome, *The Babylonian Captivity of the Church*. In this work, Luther compared the current state of the church to Israel's exile in Babylon. Luther went beyond previous grievances. Now he took on the sacraments, particularly the meaning of the Lord's Supper. He complained that in the Catholic understanding, the Mass repeated the sacrifice of Christ. The whole concept of the ritual emphasized the work performed by the priest. Also, because the church believed the bread and wine literally become the body and blood of Christ, a belief known as transubstantiation, laity were denied the cup lest they spill it. Therefore, the bread was placed on the tongues of congregants, and the priest drank the cup on their behalf.

Luther called it all an outrage. He recommended the Mass be spoken in the language of the people rather than Latin so worshipers could understand. He argued that laity be allowed to receive *both* the bread and cup. He also called for modifications in the symbolism, meaning primarily a less literal interpretation of the body and blood of Christ. The word we use for Luther's understanding of what happens in Communion, *consubstantiation*, means that Christ's real presence was in the meal but did not change the properties of the bread and cup. This would become a point of contention with other reformers like Huldrych Zwingli, who held that the elements of Communion were merely symbolic of Christ's presence.

Many historians believe that had Luther stuck with indulgences as his point of issue, there may never have been a divide in the church, but when he ventured into the sacraments, the separation became fixed. As Luther's friend and fellow theologian, Erasmus, said after reading *Babylonian Captivity*, "The breach is irreparable."

This led to a papal bull, or decree, in 1520 requiring Luther to appear before a tribunal, giving him the chance to recant his words or else be convicted as a heretic, meaning he could be put to death. After much political maneuvering, the assembly, called a Diet, convened in Worms in the spring of 1521.

Luther was pointedly asked by King Charles, the Holy Roman Emperor, "Will you recant?"

After taking a night to think about his response, Luther came back the next day and said these words: "I cannot and will not recant anything, for to go against conscience is neither right nor safe." Scholars debate the veracity of Luther's next words, but they are part of popular tradition. "God help me. Here I stand. I cannot do otherwise."

What happened next?

You'll have to turn to chapter 5 to find out, but not just yet! This is a very critical moment in Luther's life and the Protestant Reformation. It's as if centuries of daring steps taken by theologians and pastors came to this moment. Luther declared himself, and because he was the right voice at the right time, the scales tipped. This is a place worth pausing to consider the significance of what it means to take stands in our own faith.

Keys to Taking a Stand

Jackie Robinson was the first African American to break the color barrier in Major League baseball. His courage is legendary. He faced despicable abuse from fans and players alike, but he was also encouraged by the stands some teammates took. One of them was PeeWee Reese, the all-star shortstop for the Dodgers.

In Robinson's rookie season in 1947, the Dodgers were playing a series at Cincinnati, near Reese's native Kentucky. When the Dodgers took the field in the bottom of the first, amidst abusive heckling from the stands, Reese walked over to Robinson at first base. In a scene depicted in the movie *42*, Reese put his arm on Robinson's shoulder and told him, "Thank you, Jackie." When Robinson asks what Reese is thanking him for, Reese points up to the crowd and says, "I've got family up there from Louisville. I need 'em to know. I need 'em to know who I am."[1]

Of course, we don't know what Reese actually said to Robinson. Neither man ever quoted the words, but several people witnessed the scene. Just the image of Reese running over to speak with Jackie and putting his arm on Jackie's shoulder was enough.

> *If our stands tell people*
> *who we are, what do people*
> *know about you? Our words*
> *and actions either confirm*
> *our creeds or betray them.*

If our stands tell people who we are, what do people know about you? Our words and actions either confirm our creeds or betray them. Of course, no one is perfect. As the hymn says, "Though what I dream and what I do / in my weak days are always two, / help me, oppressed by things undone, / O thou whose deeds and dreams were one!"[2] We all have to live with the gap between creeds and deeds, but our gaps are a microcosm of the world's gaps. As long as the patterns of this world do not conform to the will of God revealed in the life of Jesus, there will be stands required.

We are seeing people take very defining stands in our world today from Black Lives Matter to the Me-Too Movement to the Never Again Movement. What compels us is not our courage but the cause.

What can we learn from our Reformation history and biblical examples about taking stands in our faith? Let's answer that question with some questions.

How Does My Stand Align with God's Will?

It begins with asking how the stand I feel called to take lines up with what God wants for this world. Inevitably that will involve matters of justice and peace and respect for all people.

Sometimes we have to stand up for ourselves. That may be the hardest stand for some to take, standing up for yourself when you are treated unfairly.

Other times it means standing up for others who are mistreated. We are called to take a stand for those no one stands up for. Jesus didn't take a stand to improve his own standing but to put others in good standing before God.

A member of our staff, Jeanne Lewis, has a fifteen-year-old daughter. She recently shared with me a paper her daughter wrote for a high school English assignment. It is an open letter to her classmates:

> As your peer, it's probably inappropriate to think I have any right to tell you how to conduct yourselves. I am not your parent, your teacher, or even your older sibling. For many of you I am not an acquaintance. However, a time comes when the people who should be guiding you are not telling you the truth. A time comes when one notices far too many injustices and must take a stand. This is my stand.

She continues with an impassioned plea to her classmates to stop racism. She calls people out for embedding racism in humor and making assumptions about those from different ethnic backgrounds. She asks them—she *tells* them—in no uncertain terms, to stop.

That is a stand that clearly lines up with the character and example of Jesus. When we stand against prejudice and bullying, we stand with Jesus. When we stand up to those who perpetuate discriminatory views, we stand with Jesus. When we stand with people who are unfairly treated, we stand with Jesus.

What Happens If I Don't Take this Stand?

Martin Luther King Jr. once preached a sermon on the good Samaritan. He pointed out the way Jesus forever changed the

74

perceptions of Samaritans because of one story. The Samaritan defined goodness by the way he changed an important question. The priest and Levite who did not help the victim were most concerned about what would happen if they did. But the Samaritan asked a different question, says King. What happens if I do *not* help him?[3]

What happens if we remain silent? What happens if we go along with the crowd? What happens if we try to avoid needs we can do something about? What happens if we keep things the way they are and refuse to learn or dialogue about an issue or consider changes that could honor God?

I remember watching on television the student revolt in Tiananmen Square in Beijing, China, in 1989. The scene captivated me because I had been in Tiananmen Square exactly one year prior when I traveled there while serving a church in England. I watched in amazement as a lone student held his ground in front of a cavalry of tanks. In fact, when the lead tank tried swerving around him, the student would move to keep it from passing. He was clearly saying, "If you want to go further, you'll have to go through me!" The tanks came to a halt.

Do you think that student stood there because he thought he was going to win? Of course not! You don't stand in front of a tank and win. But I also doubt he stood his ground because he thought his actions alone would change things. He had the demeanor of someone who had simply had enough. He wasn't focused solely on what happened to him. He was sending the message that to stand and fall would be better than never having stood at all. Though many other students were demonstrating that day, this one person's action emboldened a generation and people around the world. China has certainly not been the same since. The Chinese Communist Party started drawing in the middle class, leading to significant social and economic changes making China a new superpower on the world stage.[4]

It is natural to ask when taking a risky, costly stand, what will happen to me? But it's the next question that determines our action, what happens if I don't?

What Can God Do with My Stand?

In the Gospel of John, there are three events involving Nicodemus. This first occurs in John 3, when he came to inquire of Jesus at night, waiting until darkness, which we can assume was to prevent being recognized by his colleagues. The next mention is in 7:50-52, where the religious leaders plotted against Jesus. Nicodemus spoke up and questioned the fairness of convicting someone without a trial. His colleagues mocked him. The final mention in John 19:38-42 follows the Crucifixion, but this time Nicodemus is joined by a colleague, Joseph of Arimathea, who is introduced as a secret disciple for fear of what the religious leaders would think of him. Together, at the foot of the cross, both Nicodemus and Joseph appear publicly to take a defining stand. They assume responsibility for Jesus' burial.

Looking at these details, doesn't it seem possible that Joseph came into light as a follower of Christ because he had watched Nicodemus take increasingly bolder steps? Courage is contagious. When we see boldness rising in someone acting on their God-given convictions, we get inspired.

Martin Luther nailed his 95 Theses to a church door and an entire population was energized. He spoke his mind openly in debates, and others like Bucer, Melanchthon, and Karlstadt came alongside him. Rosa Parks stood tall by taking a seat in the whites-only section of a Montgomery, Alabama, bus and fueled the civil rights movement. Nelson Mandela was exiled to Robben Island for resisting apartheid, and South Africa was galvanized to continue the fight until twenty-seven years later, when apartheid was abolished. Malala Yousafzai stood her ground against the

Taliban, believing she had a right to go to school, and she was shot in the head. Miraculously, she survived and continues to inspire the cause of women's rights around the world.

God never wastes an act of courage when that act reflects the will of God.

Who Is Standing with Me?

One final, but very important, point must be made. Few people when first approached to take a bold stand feel they are capable of doing so. When Moses was asked to go to Pharaoh and say, "Let my people go!" he responded to God, "Who am I?" When Gideon was met by an angel and asked to deliver the Israelites, he replied, "But I am the least of my people." Esther felt too afraid, Isaiah too sinful, Jeremiah too young, and Peter too flawed.

Now had they been asked, respectively, to tend sheep, thresh wheat, compete in a beauty contest, interpret visions, speak publicly, or go fishing, my guess is they would have said, "You're on!" That's because they had proven success in those areas. They could rely on their ability. A God-assignment is different. Our ability will play a part but not the only part. We will have to depend on supernatural help. We will most likely have to do things we don't feel confident to complete. Heavenly reliance becomes the key trait, which means our self-reliance will get in the way.

My preaching professor in seminary, the late Dr. Fred Craddock, took an interesting angle on the story of Peter walking on water. Caught in a storm on Galilee, the disciples were in a boat *without Jesus*. They were afraid, and when they saw Jesus walking toward them, they panicked even more, thinking he was a ghost. When Jesus told them not to be afraid, Peter invited himself to join Jesus, so Jesus bid him, "Come." Let me speed this up. Peter did, walked on water, got distracted by the wind and waves, sank, cried out to Jesus, was rescued by Jesus, and got back in the boat *with Jesus*. Dr. Craddock recognizes the infinite sermons that laud Peter's courage for stepping out of the boat. Frankly this is the angle I had always taken with this story: Peter took a bold stand and experienced a miracle. But Dr. Craddock talked about how the boat is a symbol for the church. The hope of the church is Jesus being in the boat, not the disciples trying to act like Jesus on their own!

We are all in the same boat. Our job is to seek Jesus' presence. As Jesus first told the disciples in the story, "Take courage. I am here!" (Matthew 14:27 NLT). We take courage not in our ability, but in the power of him who never leaves us or forsakes us. We stand strong because of him who stands with us. We never stand alone. Whatever the reform we feel called to make, the One who is with us is greater than anyone or anything against us.

Our steps don't have to be leaps. The greatest reforms might start with a small act of obedience. Don't focus on the difference you think your action will make. Focus on what God is stirring inside you. You never know how many others will stand because of your stand. Difficult stands are never easy, but as Robert Schuller once said, "Tough times don't last, but tough people do."

Where do you stand?

CHAPTER 5
REFUGE

CHAPTER 5
REFUGE

I can tell you in this idle solitude there are a thousand battles with Satan....Often I fall and am lifted again by God's right hand.

—Martin Luther[1]

Early in my ministry I worked as an associate pastor under a seasoned veteran senior pastor, Dr. Bernard Fitzgerald. One day while we were talking in his office, he shared with me a story from the early days of his career. Soon after completing his service in World War II, he got married and responded to a call to ministry. While serving his first church, he learned he had tuberculosis. He spent several months in the VA Hospital in Asheville, North Carolina, and was told by doctors he might never be able to pastor again.

As he was spending long days in bed, he began to get discouraged. He felt such a clear leading from God, but now it looked as though he would not be able to follow his call. One afternoon, he noticed a man wearing a mask and gown and walking from bed to bed talking with patients. Something about the man's demeanor and the way he engaged the other soldiers led Bernard to believe that he wasn't a doctor. The gentleman finally reached Bernard's bed and asked about his condition. Within minutes the story was spilling out—Bernard explained his call to ministry, entering seminary, getting sick, and finding out his career plans might change.

The man listened with interest and compassion. When the story ended, the visitor asked if he might say a prayer with Bernard. Taking his hand, the gentleman closed his eyes and said, "Lord, your servant didn't ask for this situation and he certainly can't change it by his own power, but remind him that while he is limited, you are unlimited. While he is still, you are busy. Work on his behalf so that this bed may become a sanctuary of your presence giving him an assurance that you will provide for his future just as you have his past. In Christ's name. Amen."

Bernard said in that moment he felt a rush of peace come over him. As the man got ready to walk away, Bernard realized they had not introduced themselves, so he shared his name. The man shook Bernard's hand and said, "I'm Billy Graham."

Bernard, of course, went on to have an incredible ministry even in retirement. He said he never forgot the day a stranger took time to pray at his bedside. He discovered that an unwanted exile didn't take him from his career but prepared him for it.

In this chapter, we will look at a comparatively brief but extremely significant period in the life of Martin Luther when he was forced into a time of retreat. His refusal in Worms to recant his opinions triggered threats against his life. As Newton's third law of motion says: for every action there is an equal and opposite reaction. The Vatican would now react.

Before considering Luther's exile, think for a moment about your own stands that go against established patterns. Whether you are talking about reforming city hall, the school board, your Sunday school class, or your own personal habits, it's important to recognize that reform brings resistance. Someone somewhere has an investment in things the way they are. Changing anything, yourself included, brings opposition, and opposition of any kind wears us down over time. Without periods of refuge, reform can't survive.

To begin looking at the value of refuge in Martin Luther's life, and our own, let's briefly consider a few things refuge does not mean.

What Refuge Is Not

- **Avoiding.** Sometimes getting away to a place of refuge turns into hiding. Rather than replenishing, it becomes avoiding. We find ourselves retreating to get away from things we don't want to face. This is not refuge. It is putting off responsibility.
- **Ignoring.** Sometimes we depend on people as our refuge. We go to them for support and encouragement when we are hurting or struggling, but when they tell us something we don't want to hear, we shut them out. We say they aren't safe anymore, because they tell us things we don't want to hear. If we seek trusted relationships only with those who make us feel good about ourselves, then we will never be more than we are. Proverbs 27:6 says, "Wounds from a sincere friend / are better than many kisses from an enemy" (NLT). Refuge is not ignoring truth about ourselves.
- **Quitting.** Some people have a hard time getting away from stress and pressure because taking time for self-care feels like giving up. Of course, in a sense, that is true. From time to time, we need to cease and surrender. But there is a difference between quitting

and quieting. The more demanding our reform, the more critical the need for refuge in order to be still and receive God's help.

I love the part in the Exodus story where Moses leads the people out of Egypt. They get to the edge of the Red Sea and realize Pharaoh's army has cornered them. The Israelites have nowhere to go, and they panic, regretting ever listening to Moses in the first place. Moses told them, "The LORD will fight for you; you need only to be still" (Exodus 14:14 NIV). This truth goes against every grain of our human instinct, especially in a crisis, because our nature compels us to fight harder, but that is not how we receive God's help. Divine deliverance comes from being still, and that was something Martin Luther had to learn the hard way.

A Forced Retreat?

Following the Diet of Worms, the Holy Roman Emperor, Charles V, issued the *Edict of Worms*, which declared Martin Luther a heretic. The reason he wasn't bound immediately and taken to Rome was an agreement made beforehand that, no matter what the outcome was in Worms, Luther would be allowed to return to Wittenberg. Now, however, with the declaration of this edict, a person could legally strike him down and not face consequences. In other words, it was open season on Martin Luther.

While Luther was traveling back to Wittenberg, a group of horsemen overtook his party, kidnapped him, and carried him away. Clearly, that was the end of Martin Luther...or was it? The episode was staged. Luther's kidnapping was fake news. His old friend back in Saxony, the Prince elector, Frederick the Wise, arranged for a posse to make it appear as though Luther had

Wartburg Castle

been kidnapped. Instead, they took him to Wartburg Castle for safe refuge, where Luther would spend the next ten months.

Wartburg Castle is located near the town of Eisenach, Germany, and sits atop a mountain in the beautiful Thuringian Forest. Luther called this place "the kingdom of birds," which may have been a coded way of letting his friends know where he was. To disguise himself, he quit wearing his monk's cape. He let his beard and hair grow and took the name Junker George, which in German means Sir George. This helped Luther appear like one of the knights staying at the castle.

At times, Luther's stay at the castle felt like an eternity. He called it "my Patmos," referring to the island where the Apostle John was exiled. Luther struggled with feeling he had abandoned the cause and his colleagues back in Wittenberg. Yet, as we will see, Luther wasn't idle during this time. His months at the castle proved to be extremely productive, but the real lessons from this time are not so much about Reformation history but Reformation realities.

Luther's forced period of exile at Wartburg Castle holds valuable lessons regarding the importance of refuge in the spiritual life. So much of the Bible, especially Psalms, talks about the need for refuge and how we find that in God. Refuge takes many forms. It can be a place we go daily to be alone with God. It can be an occasional place we get away to, a cabin, a retreat center, some place of exile where we can refocus. This isn't to be seen as a luxury. Refuge isn't something we take when we can afford it. Refuge is a necessity created by the tension of living between is and ought, the way things are and the way things ought to be. As people of faith, we are called to live in this tension between two worlds—the fallen, imperfect world we call home now and the world of God's completed kingdom that we will call home one day.

The church lives between these realities of the now and not yet. In some ways, you could say the church is a magnification of the individual Christian life. God accepts us as we are, but God doesn't leave us as we are. God's desire is to form us into the image of Christ. Each of us knows the grind of living between these realities, between the person we are and the person we hope to become. As Paul said, "For I do not do the good I want, but the evil I do not want is what I do" (Romans 7:19 NRSV). We are called to live with a constant tension between our present reality and future possibility.

As a collection of Christians, the church simply becomes a grand assembly of tension! The default of the human spirit is to do what satisfies the self, in other words, to reduce tension and keep life comfortable. Hence the famous last words of a church member, "We've never done it that way before!" Change brings with it fear, and fear is typically the enemy of progress. Reformers, however, don't give in to fear. The greatest fear of a reformer is not changing, becoming complacent, and forfeiting the way things could be for the way things are. Reformers are hopeless romantics, never letting go of God's dream for their lives and for the way this world could be with God's rule in effect. Bobby Kennedy described reformers when he said, "Some men see things as they are and say, why; I dream things that never were and say, why not."

Reformers disturb the status quo of church life by always asking the question *Why not?* Why not do what it takes to reach more people? Why not become multicultural? Why not stand against racism, human trafficking, poverty, or hunger? Why not dream God's dream for us in this place at this time?

Check your pulse right now. Is your heart beating faster? If so, you probably have a reformer's heart in you, but here is your caution! Living this way will be challenging. You will find yourself at odds with people you thought were friends. You will get exhausted at times. You will have days when you get discouraged and want to throw in the towel. You will need refuge. You will need to retreat in order to believe that the goal is worth the toll. Just how does that happen? Let's consider some revelations that refuge provides.

Revelation 1: God Uses What We Are Able to Do

In his early days at Wartburg Castle, Martin Luther was consumed with thoughts of all the things he wasn't doing. He wasn't providing leadership to his friends back in Wittenberg. He wasn't rallying the troops. He wasn't planning the next event to promote Reformation ideas. He wrote, "I did not want to come here. I wanted to be in the fray."[2]

But after a while, his thoughts turned to what he could do, so he began writing. He was famously known to have thrown his ink pot at the devil, which was most likely Luther's euphemistic way of saying that his response to personal spiritual torment was to write. He literally threw ink by writing hundreds of pages. In ten months he completed more than a dozen works, the most important of which was the translation of the New Testament and the Book of Psalms into German. This may have been Luther's most significant achievement. For the first time, Germans could read Scripture in their own language. Without the need of a priest to interpret a Latin Bible, God's Word had been communicated in the native tongue of Germans. Martin Marty, author and scholar of Protestant history, conjectured that "this Bible did more than any other book to begin to shape the modern German literary styles."[3] The feat, however, might never have happened were it not for Luther's period of solitude.

Luther's translation was not only a gift to multitudes at that time, but many more through the centuries following, especially one man who read it some 420 years later. Claus Westermann was a noted Lutheran pastor and theologian who in World War II served time in a prison camp. The only thing he possessed besides his clothes was Luther's New Testament and Psalms. This resource turned out to be very influential in the way Westermann faced this time. Consider his reflections on one particular experience:

There were times when you could not understand God anymore. You had to speak against God. Then I saw that this was what really happens in the Psalms....In Russian prison camp one time we stood in a circle to have a worship service. One of us was asked to pray. He read Psalm 103. We were standing with our heads bowed, stooped over. But afterward I thought, "That's not the way to praise God! Such a psalm has to be spoken with joy, your head raised, your body erect!" In that experience I learned the difference between real praise and our notion of prayer. Then I began my dissertation, writing on a little board, sometimes trading bread for

> *Part of the church's mission
> is to provide people experiences
> of refuge that do not mean
> hiding from life's hurts
> but hearing God's voice.*

paper. It was then that I discovered that the psalms of the Old Testament really come out of human experience.[4]

In his refuge, Luther focused on what he could do, and as a result, God used his words to encourage someone who four centuries later would find that his imprisonment became a refuge in which he heard God's call to ministry.

Part of the church's mission is to provide people experiences of refuge that do not mean hiding from life's hurts but hearing God's voice.

Revelation 2: God Is Actively Present

While Luther was at Wartburg Castle, other leaders of the Reformation movement began stepping up. Andreas Karlstadt, who was serving as pastor of the Castle Church in Wittenberg, spoke the Christmas Mass in German. This was the first time the service was performed in a language other than Latin. It was also the scene of another first: the laity received *both* the bread and the cup. Also, he and other pastors stopped wearing church vestments. Karlstadt even got married!

Now all of these changes created upheaval, something Luther would have to address when he left Wartburg Castle, but when that time came, he would discover that reformation had been spreading even while he was in isolation. Years later, he would tell about his discovery of God's power to work when he was idle: "While I slept...the Word so greatly weakened the papacy that no prince or emperor ever inflicted such losses upon it. I did nothing; the Word did everything."[5] Sometimes we can't see what God is doing until we stop what we are doing.

Typically, we learn this the hard way. When we get to the place where there is nothing we can do, we experience what God can do. Have you ever been to Wartburg Castle? My Wartburg experience was not in Germany but rather on a lonely two-lane highway in northern Colorado. I had experienced two music director changes in less than three years, causing hurt and confusion in the congregation I served at the time.

Looking for a new director, I focused on a person in the community with incredible talent who had attended The Julliard School. She politely refused. Several weeks later, I contacted her again and made another offer and received yet another refusal. We then offered the position to another very qualified person, who accepted. Our choir and music teams planned a welcome reception at the church. I stopped by my office right before the gala and found a note stuck in the door. It was from the candidate-elect saying she had changed her mind. You can imagine the churning in my stomach as I explained to the assembled teams what had happened.

Thus, I went back to Ms. Julliard for one final offer. She replied with a three-page letter. She had obviously done her homework and talked with people in the congregation. She informed me that because of the "extreme division" in the church, she must decline, and this was her final answer. I thought, "I have a congregation willing to let me know they are unhappy, I don't need to hear it from a stranger!" I was at the lowest point in my career.

My wife and I had planned a vacation by ourselves that year, but she suggested I go ahead of her for a few days. Wonder why! I arrived at the airport in plenty of time to make the flight and was told my bag would not be loaded in time so I would have to wait after arriving. I was fit to be tied. I spent the first two hours of the flight writing a letter to the president of the airlines, the president of the FAA, the president of the United States, God, and anyone else responsible for this outrage.

Since I was going to southwestern Colorado, I flew into Albuquerque. After four hours, my bags arrived, and I quickly drove out of the city toward Santa Fe and then Colorado. I felt like I was late for an appointment when I realized, "Why am I hurrying?" Nothing is waiting on me. I will get there and just go to bed. Slow down."

As I drove toward the beautiful San Juan mountain range, I traveled on one of those long-deserted roads you see in western pictures, where the road descends for miles in a perfectly straight line, then ascends in equal height. The evening sun was casting a magnificent reddish glow on the mountains. I became captivated by what looked like an eagle soaring around a rock spire. It never flapped a wing, moving effortlessly in even circles.

I pulled the car off the road and sat on the hood leaning back against the windshield. With my hands behind my head, I just watched this bird soar, and something happened to me that has never happened before or since. A song came to me. Now I am not the poetic type. This was a rare moment of inspiration. I wrote down the words based on Psalm 121:1-2, "I lift up my eyes to the hills— / from where will my help come? / My help comes from the LORD" (NRSV). After a period of time, I got back in the car and completed my journey. Without explanation, all of my angst and anger were gone. I got in bed that night and felt God say, "You know, had you not been delayed, you wouldn't have had that experience."

I had a restful, rejuvenating vacation. Susan was even impressed by my revived spirit when she joined me. I didn't think about the church or worry about the problems. I returned two weeks later to find the usual stack of mail waiting on my desk. On top of it was a phone message from Ms. Julliard. I called, and she explained a very unusual experience. She awoke one morning and sat up in bed. Her husband asked if something was wrong. She said, "I feel God is telling me not to close the door on that job." As it turns out, she accepted, and over the next decade of our working together, the church more than doubled in size. She is still at that church today.

When I took refuge, God took over.

In the introduction to his translation written at Wartburg Castle, Luther said that in the Psalms "an assurance is given to us, upon which we may confidently rely, that we may without fear and hesitation follow in the footsteps of the good [saints] who have preceded us." That's sixteenth-century speak for "God's got this!"

Revelation 3: God's Strength Is More Dependable Than Our Own

Luther suffered tremendous bouts of spiritual attack at Wartburg Castle. His insecurities and physical ailments left him depressed and sick.

Perhaps the greatest torment was the way he felt taunted by the devil. Sometimes solitude has a downside. When left alone with our thoughts, our thoughts can become the enemy. He also wrote to Melanchthon, "I can tell you in this idle solitude there are a thousand battles with Satan."[6] Yet Luther's time at Wartburg Castle revealed his defense against these personal struggles.

In his study room, Luther took his knife and carved into the table, "I am baptized!" This was Luther's way of affirming his God-given identity and worth when he was assailed by the demons of doubt and despair. Luther reminded himself that he belonged to God, and just as Jesus heard, God was well pleased with him. This gave Luther strength to keep going when his own strength gave out.

Psalm 18:3 says, "All I need to do is cry to him" (TLB). In a discouraged time, we can turn to many things for relief, but nothing takes the place of God's help. Nothing else can change people's hearts. Nothing else can give supernatural comfort. Nothing else can take away fear in a moment of crisis. That's the great promise of Scripture, that God not only saves us from trouble, God also saves us in trouble. God doesn't save us from death. God saves us in death.

Martin Luther King Jr. once told a story from the early days of the Montgomery bus boycott. Mother Pollard was one of the most committed workers in the bus protest. She was poor and uneducated, but in spite of that she was very intelligent and insightful. She worked hard for the movement, and even though she was physically exhausted, she often remarked that her soul was at rest.

One Monday night, King spoke at a rally after a tense week in which he had been arrested and received numerous death threats. He attempted to convey strength and courage to everyone, and perhaps did for most people, but not Mother Pollard. After the event, she motioned for King to come to her. She hugged him, asking what was wrong, and could not be fooled by King's attempts to convey he was fine. She told him, her face radiant: "God's gonna take care of you."

These simple words consoled King, giving him courage in the moment. He would recall them to bring him hope, peace, and guidance through the troubles and tribulations he would inevitably bear. "This faith transforms the whirlwind of despair into a warm and reviving breeze of hope," he said after describing his interaction with Mother Pollard in his book *Strength to Love*. He then referenced an ancient proverb about finding strength in faith, describing the need for all devout people to take to heart: "Fear knocked at the door. Faith answered. There was no one there."[7]

Accessing such strength may be simple, but that doesn't mean it's simplistic. Two Martin Luthers nearly half a millennium apart affirm the same truth: reformation needs refuge.

CHAPTER 6
THE PRIESTHOOD
OF ALL BELIEVERS

CHAPTER 6
THE PRIESTHOOD OF ALL BELIEVERS

The place God calls you to is the place where your deep gladness and the world's deep hunger meet.
—Frederick Buechner

God is milking the cows through the vocation of the milkmaid.
—Martin Luther

Wayne Cordeiro is the gifted pastor of New Hope Christian Fellowship in Honolulu. I once heard him speak at a conference where he had two people take a piece of string and walk in opposite directions until they disappeared off stage. He invited the audience to imagine the string as eternity, no beginning or end. Then he grabbed one point of the string with his fingers and invited people to think of the place, a single dot on the line, as their lives. In the span of eternity our lives are but dots on a line that goes forever.

Cordeiro said most people live their lives squeezing everything they can out of their dot. They make the most of every moment, hoping to extend their dot as long as possible. They even ask God to lighten the difficulties of their dot, prolong their dot, and fill their dot with as many good things as possible, but in the end our lives are still just dots. He suggests that the quality of our dot is not determined by how much we pack into it, but what we get out of it. Instead of seeking the resources of eternity to serve our dot, fulfillment in life is found in using the resources of our dot to serve eternity.

This may be the Protestant Reformation's most important contribution to the church: rediscovering the eternal value of our dots. After all, our spiritual DNA means we are programmed to see our vocation (we'll come back to that word) as allowing God to use our lives to give God glory. This is what scripture teaches. The disciples were ordinary people who followed Jesus. They had no special training or education for ministry, except of course, following Jesus for three years! Once they were empowered by the Holy Spirit on the Day of Pentecost to carry on Jesus' work, the church was born.

The Apostle Paul wasn't trained as a church strategist, yet his principles were a master plan for church growth and health. In his letters to the Corinthians, Romans, and Timothy, he described the way God gives gifts to all people. Every member of the church has a part to play in carrying out God's purpose in the world. My evangelism professor, Dr. George Morris, used to say that instead of showing the names of hired clergy on church signs, there should be a line that reads: "Ministers: All the Members of the Church!" The hiring of ministers was the beginning of church decline.

This was the thesis for a paper I wrote in seminary. I went to school in the mid-1980s, about the time The United Methodist Church started facing the reality of its decline in membership and attendance. My thesis was to identify the origins of this decline and the lessons for us today. The peak of Methodism in America was around the turn of the twentieth century, when it was the largest religious movement in the country. During this time, few churches had pastors. They were grouped in geographic regions served by circuit riders—trained, sometimes ordained, pastors who went from parish to parish on horseback. (Congregations were often identified as parishes, meaning they saw their ministry target as the community around them, not just the members of the church!)

An individual congregation might not see its pastor for months. When the pastor visited, it was not to do ministry, but rather ministry training. The weekly preaching, teaching, and calling on people was done by volunteers in the absence of trained clergy. As I studied statistics and historical records, I came to the conclusion that as a denomination, Methodism started declining when circuit riders settled down and single churches began hiring pastors to lead their individual congregations. Instead of doing the work of the church, the laity became spectators receiving ministry performed by professional clergy. In other words, we cultivated "pew potatoes."

There is a humorous story about the way the tradition of circuit riders got started. John Wesley, the founder of Methodism, was adamantly opposed to non-ordained clergy preaching. On one occasion when an assigned clergy was delayed in arriving to preach to his Methodist gathering in London, a layman stood and delivered the sermon. When Wesley found out, he bolted for London to reprimand the wayward preacher. Wesley's mother, who was in attendance at the service, intervened and said to her son, "He is as called of God to preach as you are!"

Wesley changed his mind and circuit riding preachers quickly populated...and Methodism flourished!

I don't remember the grade I got on that paper, but I do remember the education I received in my first appointment. I served two small churches with fewer than 100 people in worship attendance combined! I typed, printed, and folded the bulletins. I did all the hospital and shut-in visitation. I was expected to visit every member at least annually. I led all of the services except to direct the choirs, and I even did that on one occasion! Never mind the fact that I had no musical background. That was hardly a prerequisite!

I was young enough to keep from getting exhausted by the work, but I had an inner conviction that this was not the best way to do church. The sum of my ministry became a tiring routine of keeping congregants happy. Success was not measured in growth of new people, giving, or quality of preaching and education. I received no annual evaluation assessing how well I met intended goals. My approval was based purely on the straw poll of people who did or didn't like me. I knew there must be a better way.

Martin Luther's reclaiming the biblical principal of the priesthood of all believers is perhaps as radical now as it was in sixteenth-century Europe. Helping longtime church members see themselves as ministers can still be controversial. In this final chapter, we will study the background of this important Reformation principle and why it is vital for the life of every congregation and Christian.

When Luther Returned from the Wartburg Castle

In the early days of the Reformation, Martin Luther's thoughts and writings turned from theological ideas to the practical matters of church life. This was prompted by the needs arising in churches that were putting Reformation preaching into practice, starting in Wittenberg. During the ten months Luther spent at the Wartburg castle, chaos broke out in the city he now called home. Andreas Karlstadt, the pastor of the Castle Church, started making radical changes. Luther's colleague, Philip Melanchthon, was a brilliant theologian who helped Luther shape Reformation beliefs, but he was a weak leader. So much change and removal of order in worship was causing upheaval. The abandonment of customary patterns in church affairs was beginning to have impact on civil affairs.

A group of self-proclaimed prophets from the regional town of Zwickau came to Wittenberg. They preached against all order in the church, but even more dangerously, they used Luther's ideas to stir up peasant rebellion. The leader of this movement was Thomas Muntzer, a fiery preacher who at first supported Luther's ideas but then turned them in a political direction. By 1524 he led what came to be known as the German Peasants' War in which up to 100,000 peasants were killed. Muntzer was tortured and executed for his part.

The seeds of rebellion that were being sown during Luther's stay at the Wartburg brought him out of hiding. First, he visited Wittenberg in disguise to assess the conditions for himself. Luther had a mixture of delight and shock. He was pleased to see his ideas taking root while he was away, but the spirit of change concerned him greatly. The efforts to remove Catholic influences and set people free from restrictive traditions were often done in a spirit of intimidation and fear. Luther wondered if the effort to remove old legalisms was creating new ones.

Luther's colleagues were not proving capable of maintaining peace and order in the midst of the changes. Melanchthon was ineffective at dealing with the Zwickau prophets, and Karlstadt, the pastor of the Castle Church, was becoming a renegade himself, adding fuel to the fire of rebellion.

Soon after he returned to Wartburg Castle, the city council of Wittenberg sent a message to Luther pleading with the exiled leader to come home and restore order. Thus, starting on the first Sunday in Lent, Luther preached a series of sermons at the St. Mary's Church, or City Church. These came to be known as the *Invocavit Sermons* (*Invocavit* means the First Sunday in Lent). The basic theme of these sermons was law and gospel. Luther, "the free one," the champion of grace, now spoke of the role of law and responsibility laid upon the Christian whose life had been liberated by God's grace. He preached about a doctrine called the priesthood of all believers, a concept he first described a few years earlier in a pamphlet titled *Address to the Christian Nobility of the German Nation*.

In some ways, this doctrine was born out of a very practical outcome of Luther's theology reflected in changes to worship practices. In that time, people didn't sit on pews during services, except the very wealthy members of the church. Most stood through the entire Mass, which could last two to three hours. (Perhaps a good reminder today for people who complain if a service goes a few minutes past the hour!) We remember from chapter 2 that the altar table was placed against the wall. That meant that for much of the service, the priest's back was to the congregation as he faced the altar. In performing the sacrifice of the Mass, the priest was representing the people before God.

Since Luther taught that the Mass was not a work by which we receive forgiveness but a recognition of the grace of Christ offered through the meal, the people did not need someone standing between them and Christ. Therefore, the table was pulled out from the wall. The priest stood behind the table facing the congregation so that there was nothing between the people and Christ. In other words, the people were now the ones facing the table. They were participants in the service. They were priests! This was the priesthood of all believers.

This meant, of course, that the people had to act like priests. The people had a responsibility. They were to be priests for one other.

Gospel and Law Belong Together

When Luther returned to Wittenberg with the town in upheaval and people casting off ecclesiastical restraint, he mounted the pulpit and began preaching that law and gospel belong together. This must have been surprising to his listeners. Just a few years prior, Luther's spiritual breakthrough came as a result of understanding that law (or works) does not get us into heaven. We are saved by grace alone. Now he hammered the understanding that grace doesn't mean lawlessness. Grace is not a license to do as we please, but to do as God pleases.

Luther said, "Good works do not make a man good, but a good [person] does good works."[1] His simple point is that while we don't do works to earn our salvation, when we have accepted God's grace, that grace gives us a responsibility. We do good things for God out of our love for God. These sermons restored order to the town.

The combination of law and gospel is what keeps Christianity balanced. If we focus too much on law, we make our works the source of salvation. We are back to earning God's approval and grace means little. If we focus too much on gospel, we become negligent and even irresponsible in facing the problems of this world. As the old saying goes, some people are so heavenly minded that they are no earthly good. What are ways you maintain this balance?

A New Understanding of Vocation

Another implication of the doctrine of the priesthood of all believers is the understanding of the word *vocation*. In Luther's

> *For Luther, all Christians are*
> *on equal footing with one another.*
> *Our differences are*
> *not in status but in the ways*
> *we serve one another.*

time, *vocation* had a very exclusive meaning. It was equated with calling, specifically God's calling to holy orders such as the priesthood or other professional offices in the church. *Vocation* comes from the Latin word *vocare*, meaning "to listen," or in a spiritual sense, "to hear God call us," much like Jesus heard God's voice at his baptism, "You are my Son, whom I love; with you I am well pleased" (Mark 1:11 NIV). Vocation came to be understood in this purely sacred sense and was reserved for roles within the church.

Luther blew this concept wide open. He said we all have vocations. Just as Jesus was baptized, all baptized people are called by God and given a job to do, but those jobs are not just church jobs. He used to say that the person milking the cow or the farmer working in the field carry out their ministry as much as the priest in church. He said, "This word *priest* should become as common as the word Christian."[2] For Luther, all Christians are on equal footing with one another. Our differences are not in status but in the ways we serve one another.

These simple understandings have had huge implications for Christians ever since. They have huge implications for your life and mine today.

"Little Christs"

Luther's expression for the role of every Christian was that they should be "little Christs." First Peter 2:9 states, "But you are…a royal priesthood, a holy nation, God's special possession, that you may declare the praises of him" (NIV). Pay particular attention to the words *possession* and *declare*. First, we are to be possessed by Christ. We are to be full of his spirit. To be possessed by something is to be controlled by another. We are to let Christ have control of us.

Then we are to declare his praises. What does that look like? If you think of a pastor in a pulpit, then you are still working with a sixteenth-century notion of vocation. There are many ways to declare God's praises. As the saying attributed to Francis of Assisi advises, "Preach the Gospel at all times. When necessary, use words." Everything we do can become a ministry. When we are at work, we can become a little Christ to a client, colleague, patient, or student. When we go to the store, we can be a little Christ to the attendant or a fellow customer. When we walk through our neighborhood, we can be a little Christ to the people who live around us.

It means becoming an outlet of the love of Christ that possesses us, and, like Christ, letting that love show forth even when rejected. One young man, described in Adam Hamilton's book *Christianity's Family Tree*, took this calling seriously with a woman who lived in his neighborhood. She frequently complained to people about this man and his children. She even called the city officials to complain that he didn't have an extension on one of his downspouts, allowing too much water to drain onto her property. Showing God's love to this woman was not easy. But when her husband died, "the young man went to the funeral. He prayed daily for her. He began mowing her lawn. He reported that mowing the woman's lawn became a source of blessing to him" as he simply looked for ways to be a servant. In the course of time, the woman's attitude toward this man changed radically due to his ministry to her.[3] Interestingly, the Latin word for priest is *pontifex*, which means bridge-builder.

St. Teresa of Avila is often quoted as saying, "Christ has no body on earth but yours, no hands but yours, no feet but yours. Yours are the eyes through which Christ's compassion for the world is to look out. Yours are the feet with which he is to go about doing good; And yours are the hands with which he is to bless us now."

When we take the call to become "little Christs" seriously, we discover that duty becomes a gift. This is where our translation from German to English robs us of meaning. Luther used a play on words here. The word *gift* in German, *die Gabe*, is part of the word for duty or responsibility, *aufgabe*. Luther pointed out that within the understanding of duty is the element of gift.

A member of our church illustrates this well. He's a counselor and was asked recently if he would help lead a ministry for people going through grief. He called one Monday night shortly after the group finished. He said, "I want to thank you for the opportunity to lead this group."

I replied, "Thank me? I want to thank you!"

He said,

> No, I want you to understand that when I was first asked, I accepted reluctantly. I thought only about the fact that this would mean giving up a free night. Tonight's session changed my perspective. Members of the group shared about their loss and the help and hope this group was giving them after just a few weeks. It just restored the feeling that God is using me, and it's the greatest thing in the world. Thank you.

Duty became a gift.

See All We Do as Ministry

This could be called the ministry of the ordinary. Ministry isn't limited just to work in the sacred sphere. It's like the young farmer who looked up in the clouds and saw the sign *PC*. He took it to be a sign from God telling him to "Preach Christ." But after a year of struggling in seminary, a fellow student offered the suggestion that *PC* might have meant Plant Corn!

Luther would say it is just as holy to plant corn as to preach Christ, provided we can see the impact on people through our work. This is why Luther often used examples from the most ordinary places of life, the maid milking the cow, the farmer baling straw, the mother changing diapers or doing laundry. Luther wanted to make the point that in these acts, there was service to other people taking place.

Sometimes it is so easy to look at what we do as a chore, or a drudgery, but what if we saw the people impacted through our work, no matter what the work is, and focused on them and how they were being served? How might that change our attitude about what we do? All is ministry according to Luther.

Brother Lawrence practiced this. He was a simple Catholic monk who lived in France about a century after Martin Luther. His task was to work in the kitchen of the monastery. Most of his chores were not glamorous. He could have easily felt that this was not how he envisioned serving God. Instead he looked for God's presence in his everyday, mundane, ordinary chores. He sought God's presence as much when he peeled carrots as he did in worship. As a result, he developed an incredible peace; another result was that his fellow monks began seeking his advice. His simple counsel became a book that is still considered a classic today, *The Practice of the Presence of God.*[4]

Our world tempts us to turn our work into an idol and make what we do about our need for success or recognition. But the

Brother Lawrence model of contentment is based on seeing everything we do, no matter how common or ordinary, as a way to honor God.

Focus on Our Source of Life, Not Success in Life

The next verse in the passage is telling. After saying that as Christians we are a royal priesthood...God's special possession to declare God's praises, we are told, "Once you were less than nothing; now you are God's own" (1 Peter 2:10 TLB). It's hard to be less than nothing. Of course, we recognize that this is not a practical description but an emotional one. We can't imagine nothing, but we may understand what it's like to feel that way.

Perhaps you have had times in life when there was nothing to look forward to, or you felt your life amounted to nothing. *Nothing* is the loneliest of words. We were on our own to find satisfaction and that led to nothing, nothing we wanted at least. We were like Luther, using every ounce of willpower to feel accepted by God and always coming up short. His efforts led to nothing, until...God's grace broke through like a military offensive. That grace did more than put him at rest. It put him to work. Luther was free to use his gifts to be a blessing, not to merit a blessing.

Nothing, if you can imagine that, replaces the worth we receive in Christ. Nothing, says Paul, separates us from the love of God in Jesus Christ (Romans 8:38-39). Once nothing stands in our way of full acceptance, we have everything to live for. We are not driven by a dependence on God to bless the things we do so that we might be successful in the eyes of other people. We are free from such comparisons and standards to be the person God wants us to be. We are free to make our life's ambition living for Christ; to awake each morning and pray, "God how may I honor you today? Show me those to whom I can be your hands of compassion and speak your words of encouragement. Use me for something." At the end of a day, if we can identify one way we sought to let God use us for others, then we had a great day. Our worth is not found in our success but in our Source of living.

Let's close this chapter by returning to Honolulu. One of the campus pastors of New Hope Christian Fellowship is a man named Elwin Ahu, a former state judge in Hawaii. His choice to leave a promising legal career to become a pastor is the result of a church that demonstrates what it means to be a priesthood of all believers.

I had the privilege of meeting Rev. Ahu and talking with him about his change, which was more spiritual than professional. While becoming quite successful as a judge, his personal life was tanking. His drive and stubbornness were costing him in the relational world, a reality made apparent by his second divorce. Drinking more than he should, he was beginning to question the future and whether this was the life he had worked so hard to attain.

An office assistant had given him a cassette tape (yes, this story is a couple of years old) that he kept tossing around the seat of his car. One day he decided to listen. He heard a sermon by Wayne Cordeiro and was brought to tears while driving. He felt that in describing what a broken life looks like, the pastor was talking about him. He decided to try the church for himself. The church worships in a high school auditorium, and he was put off before entering. A woman greeting at the door hugged everyone with a hearty, "Aloha, welcome to New Hope!" He tried squeezing by her, but no such luck. She grabbed him from behind and hugged him in spite of his arms-by-the-side response.

As he looked for a seat, he continued to be annoyed by the upbeat music and singing. "What kind of church is this?" he asked himself. Then came the sermon, and his mood was

> *When we are willing*
> *to become nothing,*
> *we discover the One who*
> *makes us something.*

changed. Again, he felt the pastor speaking right to him. He returned again and again, until deciding to take the step of volunteering. Each week, the church talked about being a community of servants where everyone serves. Worshiping at a high school required a vast amount of volunteer help to convert the campus into a church. One Sunday, Ahu signed up to serve the following weekend. This was when the real impact occurred.

As a church, New Hope believes the spirit in which service is done is as important as the service that is done. They feel that serving changes hearts, and changed hearts change the world. Ahu arrived on a Friday night to help the teams begin the weekend preparation. He was assigned to clean the boys' restrooms. He was given a toilet brush and told to scrub around the toilets. He was told the schools can only afford minimal cleaning and while wanting to have as clean a facility for church, they also want the school to benefit.

On his hands and knees scrubbing around a high school toilet, this state judge paused. Suddenly he felt God speak to him as clearly as he ever had. Jesus said, "Elwin, this is what I am doing for you. I am scrubbing away the dirt around your heart so I can give you a new one." Perhaps you've heard stories of people praying to the porcelain God, but that toilet literally became an altar. He welcomed Christ into his heart and soon after was baptized. Not much later, he resigned his position on the bench to go to work at the church. Today he is the pastor of Metro Christian Church in Honolulu.

When we serve others, we experience the One who came not to be served but to serve and give his life as a ransom. When we are willing to become nothing, we discover the One who makes us something.

We Are in a 500th Year!

We close our study with Martin Luther just approaching mid-life. The following afterword shares a few more key events in Luther's life and the Protestant Reformation, but these chapters capture the movement's main themes and contributions. These themes continue to have application to the needs and opportunities the church faces today. As mentioned in the opening of the book, if anything living is to continue serving a purpose, then it must be reformed. Just as Martin Luther never intended to start a new church but rather to reform the existing one, so may we reform and improve the church today.

In Phyllis Tickle's 2008 book, *The Great Emergence: How Christianity Is Changing and Why*, she makes the case that every 500 years, there is major reform in the church. Toward the end of the first 500 years, the church moved its headquarters to Rome, establishing Christianity in Western culture. Five hundred years later was the Great Schism, dividing the church between Orthodox Christianity in the East and Roman Catholicism in the West. Roughly 500 years later was the Reformation, which launched the Protestant Church, allowing for the unintended outcome of 45,000 Christian denominations in the world today.

Now, says Tickle, we are in another 500th year. Reform is happening again. Worship changes have brought upheaval to the church. The digital age has changed society and communities of faith alike. The rapid pace of change in media impacts the way people experience community and therefore faith. God's purposes haven't changed, but the way the church fulfills its mission must. What does a New Reformation look like to you? Some pastors and leaders are hanging on until retirement, grateful they will get out with a pension and not have to face what feels like a tidal wave of change. Others accept changes with a spirit of helpless despair.

There is no change in our world that God is unable to handle. If our history teaches anything, it is that God is always on the lookout for those bold leaders of faith willing to take a hammer and nail and declare their commitment to change the world for God's sake. The good news may have been around a while, but it's not old news. Many need to experience the Savior's love. Everyone needs purpose and meaning. No matter how many communication devices get sold this year, people still need connection.

The church has hope to offer.

AFTERWORD

Luther lived a good quarter-century beyond average life expectancy. Yet even then he packed centuries into his living. He published hundreds of works, married and had a family, continued his many disputes with Rome as well as other Reformation figures, and somewhere in the middle of it all managed to start a new branch of Christendom. In this Afterword, we will summarize the many aspects of Luther's life not covered in the previous chapters, starting with the personal.

Family Life

Though many Protestant priests like Karlstadt were officially marking their breach with Rome by getting married, Luther was resigned to a life of celibacy (not surprising for someone who became a monk!). However, he did find himself in the role of playing cupid after orchestrating the escape of a group of nuns who renounced their vows. This was very dangerous for both parties since it was considered a crime for a monk or nun to abandon their oaths to the church. Remember, this was a time when the line between church and state was often indistinguishable. And the women would have most likely been rejected by their families had they tried to return. Luther had little choice but to find suitable husbands for the women.

Legend has it that this particular group of nuns made their way to Wittenberg hiding in barrels once used to contain goods.[1] Luther was successful in securing matches for all of the former nuns except one, Katherine von Bora. She rejected each of Luther's candidates, finally identifying the one person she would accept, Luther himself! Much to the surprise of his colleagues, at the age of forty-two, Martin Luther married Katie, as he affectionately called her.

Though Luther found it disconcerting to wake up in the morning and see pigtails on the pillow, he enjoyed family life. Due to the threat of the Peasants' War and an outbreak of plague, the university for the most part, and the monastery entirely, were abandoned. Frederick the Wise gave the monastery to the Luthers as a home that eventually became known as Lutherhaus. Katherine managed the financial affairs, ran the household, and made their own beer. The Luthers had six children, and Martin enjoyed singing to the children and celebrating the holidays. One rumor is that Martin Luther started the tradition of bringing a tree into the home at Christmastime.

As the university repopulated, Lutherhaus became a favorite gathering spot for students. Following evening meals, Luther would hold court on any number of topics. Some of the students wrote and published these sayings in a collection appropriately titled Table Talks. Lutherhaus became a home-away-from-home for many of these students as the Luthers modeled family devotion and hospitality. Luther once famously advised wives to "make your husband glad to cross his threshold at night," and for husbands to "make your wife sorry to have you leave."[2] The model of a loving husband and father was a surprising part of Luther's legacy.

Social Reformer

An unintended outcome, at least in the early days of the Reformation's emphasis on reading Scripture, was the impact on education. Translating the Bible into German spurred the need for more schools to teach children how to read. This became a passion of Luther's. He said, "When schools flourish, all flourishes," and urged every town to have a school as laid out in his tract of 1524, "To the Councilmen of All Cities in Germany That They Establish and Maintain Christian Schools."

In a time that offered no school system for the general population and when education was a privilege of the wealthy and elite, Martin Luther launched an education reform. He was particularly interested in providing girls the opportunity to go to school. One of his last acts before he died was to start a girls' school in his hometown of Eisleben, located beside the St. Andrew's Church where Luther preached his last sermon. The school is still in operation today.

Luther was one of the first proponents of public education that provided schooling for all children regardless of gender or wealth. As former Catholic institutions became Protestant, he encouraged the transformation of monasteries into schools in order to provide teaching space for the increasing numbers of children. Protestants since Luther have followed his example of championing education. One of John Wesley's first social initiatives in the early days of the Methodist movement was to start the Kingswood School in Bristol, England, so underprivileged children could get an education. In more recent times, Frank Laubach, Protestant missionary to the Philippines, became known as "The Apostle to the Illiterates," giving his life to the advancement of education and founding the Each One Teach One literacy program.

Antisemitism

Now for the unflattering mark on Luther's record. Just a few years before his death, Luther wrote a scathing anti-Semitic attack titled *On the Jews and Their Lies*. By any standard, it is appalling. Luther encouraged Christians to set fire to synagogues and Jewish schools, level their houses, and remove their sacred writings. He even urged that "safe conduct on the highways be abolished completely for the Jews." Luther's words make Nazi propaganda sound mild.

About a year before the 500th Reformation anniversary, my wife, Susan, and I attended an off-Broadway play with some friends in New York. It was titled *Martin Luther on Trial*, an unwonted reflection on Luther's life to say the least. The play depicted Luther on trial in heaven. The devil was the prosecutor and Luther's wife played the defense attorney. Various figures from history were presented as witnesses.

The play took an unusual twist when Adolf Hitler took the stand. He explained that his anti-Jewish hatred was the result of his German heritage going back to Martin Luther. While not denying that animosity toward the Jews fueled the Nazi cause, Hitler credited Luther's influence for planting the seeds he merely watered. Now whether or not the play overexaggerated this truth, it left the disturbing question as to how someone who so bravely stood for Christ could in any way be associated with one of the most evil regimes in modern history.

Well, understanding history helps. First, Luther's personal history paints a very different picture. Over twenty years prior, in 1523, Luther wrote *That Jesus Christ Was Born a Jew*. He rebutted Catholics who had been unfair in their treatment of

Jews. He wrote, "If we really want to help them, we must be guided in our dealings with them not by papal law but by the law of Christian love.... If some of them should prove stiff-necked, what of it? After all, we ourselves are not all good Christians either."[3]

Luther's aim was to be an appealing witness to Jews hoping for their conversion. Given Jewish-Catholic tensions, Luther believed his separation from Catholicism would make it likely that Jews would convert to the Reform movement. When that didn't happen, Luther's deeper, historical prejudice took hold.

This leads to a second historical observation. Antisemitism has deep roots in Germany. On a cornerstone some ten feet high on an exterior wall of the City Church in Wittenberg is a vulgar image. It is a sculpted relief depicting people with pigs in such a way as to suggest that Jews are the offspring of the two. This relief, visible to all who pass by, was in place when Luther started the Protestant Church in the same building.

Like all of us, Luther was a product of his day. To live in a religious environment that condoned and saw little problem with holding such prejudice toward another group does not excuse Luther's hateful diatribe, but it helps to understand it. Disappointed by his lack of success in converting Jews, and perhaps knowing his time was growing short, Luther may have lashed out as a last-ditch effort to coerce Jews into converting to Christianity, albeit Luther's brand of Christianity.

Perhaps Luther felt that such conversions would authenticate his movement by succeeding where the Roman Church failed. Some say Luther never meant for his words, which, of course, stand in stark contrast to his earlier writings, to be taken literally. Who was the true Luther? We may never know, but the disparity points out a truth each of us probably understands. We are all mysteries to ourselves at times as we seek to live up to a noble character we desire to have but at other times get pulled down by a reality of influences and attitudes we have a hard time removing. Our inner demons get the best of us as they did Martin Luther. Regardless of the reasons, Luther left a dark stain on Protestant history that has been hard to remove and shall remain one of the more difficult-to-understand features of his legacy.

Beginning of Protestantism

This leads to an important question, just when did the Protestant Church begin? The answer depends on which brand of Protestantism you are talking about. The movement in Moravia under Hus had its own formation. The Swiss Reformation under Huldrych Zwingli, similarly, started independently of the German reform movement. While conversations and councils were held among these different branches to identify their places of agreement and disagreement, they each had their own points of founding. During this same time, English Reformation happened with King Henry VIII pulling away from Catholicism under uniquely different circumstances. You could say Europe experienced a Protestant explosion in the sixteenth century. Each brand included parts of their own articles of belief they liked about others, but also identified points of separation.

German, or what came to be known as Lutheran, Protestantism occurred over several years in the late 1520s. Like many other parts of this story, we have to understand the backstory, which is rife with political implications. First, Charles V, the Holy Roman Emperor, was facing invasion from Ottoman Turks in Europe bringing the threat of Muslim overthrow. This distraction became important in the unfolding drama of Protestantism's formation. Then, secondly, the emperor and the pope got into a bitter feud over the pope's siding with the King of France against the emperor. These two realities were significant backdrops to the establishment of the Reformation as an independent church.

Though the Peasants' War took a heavy toll on people, reformers established themselves as a powerful force and presence being more popular in the northern parts of the country. Churches and territorial princes began aligning themselves with Reformation principles. Individual churches began changing their worship styles, and while the *Edict of Worms* was still in force threatening punishment for anyone who sided with reformers, there was not much the empire was prepared to do to thwart its spread.

By 1526, an assembly, or Diet, was called to be held in the German city of Speyer. The emperor had hoped the result of this meeting would be the enforcement of the *Edict of Worms*. Instead, a decision was reached to allow individual territories to determine for themselves whether to enforce the edict until a general council of the church made a ruling. This accelerated the advancement of the Reformation.

Over the next few years, churches started clearly identifying themselves with the movement. This brought about a need for clarifying common practices of worship, government, and education. In visiting churches himself, Luther discovered the gaps between belief and practice. He found the behaviors of many members, most of whom were peasants, very alarming. He began writing catechisms for members and pastors. This meant that some of the lengthiest parts of worship became the announcements! Careful instruction was given for why various aspects of Christian life were important. Singing also became an important part of worship. Luther was somewhat of a musician and wrote many hymns for worship, even publishing a songbook.

Meanwhile, back at the ranch—that is, Rome—the increasing campaign of the Turks up the Danube River was causing alarm. Leading voices speculated that the Muslim rise was God's judgment on the Holy Roman Empire for allowing heretics within its realm. This, perhaps as much as any influence, led Charles V to call another Diet, again to be held in Speyer, in 1529. This time there was to be no tolerance of Reformation ideas. Territorial princes were not to be allowed freedom to side against the Catholic church, thus basically revoking the agreement three years earlier. This led to outcries of protests from reformers, thus giving them the name Protestants and resolving them to establish articles of separation from the church of Rome.

These articles were presented the following year at another Diet convened in Augsburg. The document created at this gathering of Protestant leaders became known as the Augsburg Confession, presented at the request of the emperor, who was seeking religious stability perhaps to surmount foreign threats to the empire. The Confession, largely authored by Philip Melanchthon, became the founding document of the Lutheran Church. While Martin Luther despised the denomination being named after him, what else really could it be called? The German adherents to the Reformation ideals were clearly Luther-ans!

Death

Martin Luther died in 1546, and while the last twenty-six years of his life were much quieter than the previous twenty-six, he maintained active involvement in church organization, was a devoted husband and father, and, of course, continued writing. His public ministry and compassion for others was seen even in his last days. Luther returned to his hometown of Eisleben to intercede in a dispute between mining families. In fact, this is the reason Luther was able to start a school in Eisleben. In coming to terms of reconciliation, the disputing families all agreed to help fund the school.

Grave Plaque

While there, he preached at the St. Andrew's Church, ending his sermon abruptly because he didn't feel well. Too weak to travel home, he died within a few days. His body was taken back to Wittenberg, where he was buried in the Castle Church with his grave plaque located, appropriately, beside the steps leading into the pulpit.

Given the bouts of depression and physical toll Luther's anguish took on him over the course of his life, it is a wonder he lived more than two decades beyond normal life expectancy at the time. During one period between the Diets of Speyer when Luther fretted over the organizational challenges of newly formed churches, bitter separations from people who had once been supporters, and ongoing debate with the heads of the Roman Church, Luther became so ill he thought he would die. In recovery, he wrote a hymn that more than any other is associated with Martin Luther and the Protestant Reformation, "A Mighty Fortress Is Our God." The last two stanzas from that hymn capture Luther's life and faith and seem a fitting place to conclude our study:

121

And though this world, with devils filled, should threaten to undo us,

we will not fear, for God hath willed his truth to triumph through us.

The Prince of Darkness grim, we tremble not for him;

his rage we can endure, for lo, his doom is sure;

one little word shall fell him.

That word above all earthly powers, no thanks to them, abideth;

the Spirit and the gifts are ours, thru him who with us sideth.

Let goods and kindred go, this mortal life also;

the body they may kill; God's truth abideth still;

his kingdom is forever.[4]

ACKNOWLEDGMENTS

I want to thank the staff of Abingdon Press for their support and tremendous patience, particularly Susan Salley for the way she got behind this project. Her affirmation and encouragement have been a gift. Maria Mayo is an outstanding editor who provided wonderful coaching and suggestions along the way. Being my first time working with Abingdon, the entire team made this a very enjoyable experience.

I also recognize the many contributions of my assistant, Marsha Thompson, who provides tireless support to me every day. Her help in researching, coordinating travel to film the DVD component, securing resources, and arranging interviews for this project could not be overstated.

As well, appreciation must be expressed to the wonderful staff of St. Luke's UMC, especially the worship team who first transformed the ideas in this book into incredible worship experiences. I am ever grateful to Cam Hershberger, our videographer, who did all of the filming and editing for the DVD. He has the gift of capturing spiritual experiences on film.

123

Of course, my church family, St. Luke's UMC deserves recognition for allowing me the time to write and film. They are a bold community of faith willing to reform for the sake of Christ, and it is an honor to be their pastor. Thank you for making the words "an open community of Christians..." a lived reality!

I also want to recognize the reformers in my life who taught me that doing the right thing is more important than doing things right: Dr. Horace Maness, my religion professor at Pfeiffer University; Dr. Fred Craddock, my advisor and preaching professor; Dr. Bill Mallard, who lived the theology he taught; and Rev. Jim Allred, my first pastor who was never afraid to shake things up.

Finally acknowledgment must be given to my wife, Susan, for talking through the ideas in this book and tolerating my disappearance in early mornings and late nights to retreat and type. Her patience, counsel, and unconditional love continue to reform my life for the better.

NOTES

Introduction

1   Greg Anderson, *Living Life on Purpose: A Guide to Creating a Life of Success and Significance* (San Francisco: HarperSanFrancisco, 1997), 12.

Chapter 1

1   Martin Luther, *Lectures on the Psalms (1519-21)*, in "Piety, Prayer, and Worship in Luther's View of Daily Life," by Carter Lindberg, in *The Oxford Handbook of Martin Luther's Theology*, ed. Robert Kolb, Irene Dingel, and L'ubomír Batka (Oxford, UK: Oxford University Press, 2014), 414–426 (415).

2   Angela Epstein, "Believe It Or Not, Your Lungs Are Six Weeks Old—And Your Taste Buds Just Ten Days! So How Old Is the Rest of Your Body?" *Daily Mail*, last updated October 13, 2009, http://www.dailymail.9co.uk/health/article-1219995/Believe-lungs-weeks-old–taste-buds-just-days-So-old-rest-body.html.

3   Karl Barth, *Church Dogmatics: The Doctrine of Reconciliation, Vol. IV/3.2*, trans. G. W. Bromiley, ed. G. W. Bromiley and T. F. Torrance (London: T&T Clark, 2010), 51–54.

4   Patrick Quinn, "After Devastating Tornado, Town Is Reborn 'Green,'" *USA Today Green Living* magazine, last updated April 25, 2013, https://www.usatoday.com/story/news /greenhouse/2013/04/13/greensburg-kansas/2078901/.

Chapter 2

1   Eric Kelsey, "Rare 1938 Superman Comic Book Found in US Wall Fetches $175,000," *The Independent*, June 13, 2013, http://www.independent.co.uk/arts-entertainment/books /news/rare-1938-superman-comic-book-found-in-us-wall -fetches-175000-8656667.html.

2   Ironically, where Luther stood to conduct the service was over the grave of Johannes Zacharias, the priest who carried out the execution of John Hus. Hus had warned Zacharias that there would come someone who would not be silenced. Imagine if Zacharias had said, "Over my dead body!" He would have turned out to be a prophet!

3   Roland H. Bainton, *Here I Stand: A Life of Martin Luther* (Nashville: Abingdon Press, 1978), 27.

4   Bainton, 44.

Chapter 3

1   Martin Marty, *Martin Luther: A Life* (New York: Penguin Group, 2004), 18.

2   Bainton, 32.

3   Martin Luther, *An Introduction to St. Paul's Letter to the Romans*, Luther's German Bible of 1522, trans. Rev. Robert E. Smith from *Vermischte Deutsche Schriften*, ed. Johann K. Irmischer, Vol. 63 (Heyder and Zimmer, 1854), 124–125.

Chapter 4

1   "Maybe Tomorrow We'll All Wear 42," *42*, directed by Brian Helgeland (2013; Burbank, CA: Warner Bros. Pictures).

2   John Hunter, "Dear Jesus, in Whose Life I See," *The United Methodist Hymnal* (Nashville: The United Methodist Publishing House, 1989), 468.

3   Martin Luther King Jr., "I've Been to the Mountaintop" (address delivered to Bishop Charles Mason Temple, Memphis, TN, April 3, 1968). See the transcript or listen to the audio at https://king institute.stanford.edu/king-papers/documents/ive-been-mountaintop-address-delivered-bishop-charles-mason-temple.

4   Dan Twining, "How Tiananmen Changed China—And Still Could," *Foreign Policy*, June 4, 2009, http://foreignpolicy.com /2009/06/04/how-tiananmen-changed-china-and-still-could/.

Chapter 5

1   Bainton, 191.

2   Ibid.

3   Marty, 73.

4   James Limburg, "Old Testament Theology for Ministry: The Works of Claus Westermann in English Translation," *Word & World* 1/2 (1981): 170, http://wordandworld.luthersem.edu /content/pdfs/1-2_scripture/1-2_limburg.pdf.

5   Marty, 86.

6   Derek Wilson, *Out of the Storm: The Life and Legacy of Martin Luther* (New York: St. Martin's Press, 2007), 180.

7   Martin Luther King Jr., *Strength to Love* (Minneapolis, MN: Fortress Press, 2010; text copyright 1963 Martin Luther King Jr.), 130–131.

Chapter 6

1   Bainton, 230.

2   Martin Luther, *The Epistles of St. Peter and St. Jude: Preached and Explained*, trans. E. H. Gillett (New York: Anson D. F. Randolph, 1859), 106.

3   Adam Hamilton, *Christianity's Family Tree: What Other Christians Believe and Why* (Nashville: Abingdon Press, 2007), 51.

4   The book is Brother Lawrence, *The Practice of the Presence of God, the Best Rule of a Holy Life* (New York: F. H. Revell Co., 1895).

Afterword

1   James M. Kittelson and Hans H. Wiersma, *Luther the Reformer: The Story of the Man and His Career*, 2nd ed. (Minneapolis, MN: Fortress Press, 2016), 201.

2   Bainton, 309.
3   Martin Luther, *Luther's Works: Christian in Society II*, vol. 45, ed. Walther I. Brandt (Philadelphia, PA: Fortress Press, 1962), 200–201, 229.
4   Martin Luther, "A Mighty Fortress Is Our God," trans. Frederick H. Hedge, *The United Methodist Hymnal* (Nashville: The United Methodist Publishing House, 1989), 110.